ECONOMIC REFORMS
&
INDIAN BANKING SECTOR

ECONOMIC REFORMS
&
INDIAN BANKING SECTOR

Editors
Dr. N.N. Sharma
Akhil Gautam & Sahil Mahajan

GAURAV Book Centre
Private Limited

Publisher
GAURAV BOOK CENTRE PVT LTD
ISO 9001:2008
4832/24,Prahlad Lane,S-207 Ansari
Road, Daryaganj, Delhi-110002
Ph.: 43570976, 23278261
Email: gauravbookcentre@gmail.com

Edition: 2015

ISBN: 978-93-83316-26-7

Laser Typesetting
JEE-VEE Graphics # 09911902109

Price: 945/-

Printed
JEE-VEE Graphics, Delhi

Contents

Tax System and Economic Reforms in India: Trends and Issues

Snch Lata

Assistant Professor

WRS Govt. PG College, Dehri (H.P.)

Abstract

In a developing economy like India tax occupies a strategically important place in the overall development of the country duc to its significant contribution to the national exchequer, which is ultimately spent on the overall development of different sectors of the economy. Taxes are the major sources of the Government revenue in most economies, the proceeds of which are channeled to various types of programmes, ranging from income security to those aimed at boosting productivity. The specific objectives of the research are as to addresses the vital area of best tax system, to evaluate the impact of tax reforms on Public finances of the Union and State Govt., to form a view of the effectiveness of tax reforms. The transition from a planned economy to a market economy necessitated wide-ranging tax reforms. Besides efficiency considerations, tax reforms have to address the issues of aligning tax policy to change in the development strategy. Thus, in globalizing environment tax reforms can serve a multitude of needs. They can help enhance revenue productivity, reduce economic distortions, and help to create a stable and predictable market environment.

Introduction

In the planned economy model adopted since independence, taxation was used as an instrument for reducing private consumption and transferring resources to the Government to enable it to undertake large-scale public investment in an effort to spur economic growth[1]. World over tax systems have undergone significant changes during the last 20 years as many countries across different ideological spectrum and varying level of development have undertaken reform[2]. To improve the tax intake and saving and investment rates, which are low by regional standard, a series of tax reforms have been considered in India. Their main thrust is to combine lower statutory rates with base broadening, to realize more revenues while lowering the marginal tax burden and removing distortions. This in turn foster growth[3].

Recent Reforms in Indian Tax System

The wave of tax reforms across the world that began in the mid 1980s accelerated in the 1990s motivated by a number of factors. In many developing countries, tax policy was directed to correct fiscal imbalance[4]. The need to correct fiscal imbalances and the transition from a centralized plan to a market economy were the important local factors hastening tax reforms. Difficulties in compressing expenditures necessitated that tax system reform take an important role in fiscal adjustment strategy. The transition from centrelized plan to market required the substitution of administered prices with market determined prices, the replacement of physical controls with financial controls and

---

1 Fiscal Reform in India, See: www.iosrjournals.org

2 Trends and Issues in tax policy and reform in India, See: www.ncaer.org/dowmloads/journals/ipf0506-paper2.pdf

3 The Tax system in India: Could reform spur growth? See: www.imf.org/external/pubs/ft/WP/2006/WP0693.pdf

4 Tax System reform in India: Achievements and Challenges ahead, See: www.ces.univ-paris1.fr/.../chinaIndia/INDIA%20Tax%20reform%20in%20In....

the substitution of public enterprises profits with tax revenues. Likewise, tax reforms become imperative in a globalizing environment. Enhancing competitiveness and attracting foreign investment require minimizing both efficiency and compliance costs of the tax system[5].

Tax reforms and economic policies have had a dual advantage of accelerating growth and maximizing tax revenues. The need of the hour is to ensure significant tax reforms aimed at rationalizing the current tax structure are undertaken to enhance revenue by broadening tax payer base and improving transparency of regulatory framework. With Indian economy developing rapidly and foreign players targeting untapped Indian domestic market, it's imperative for the new leadership to focus on bringing in simplification and rationalization in tax system by eliminated unwanted complexities and multiplicity of taxes. Accordingly, if tax measures advocated by the industry bodies are endorsed by the government it will go a long way in augmenting the Government's coffers, encouraging growth in industrial output and increase investment by the foreign players[6].

Evolving Need

In response to its changing developmental strategy, India's tax system, too, has been undergoing profound changes. Within the framework of a closed and heavily- planned economy, the tax system was based on multiple objectives: raising govt revenues, generating employment, increasing equity, and fostering investment in 'backward' regions. This gave rise to enormous complications and created channels for tax evasion and avoidance. Further, given its discretionary nature, the system has built- in incentive for firms to lobby for industry- specific concessions- which added even further to its complexity. While this system may have been sustainable within a closed economy, in today's

5 Tax System reform in India, See: academiccommons Columbia.edu/.../ IPD_WP_Tax_System_Reform_in_I.

6 Articles.economictimes.indiatimes.com>collection>Income Tax Act

globalizing world, it is more critical than ever to put in place an efficient tax system. An open-economy presents bigger challenge in setting tax rates- since there are fewer 'degree of freedom' available to policy makers. In such an environment, not only do tax rates impact foreign investment, but they can also shift the incidence of taxation in unexpected ways. Hence, being a larger and complex economy, India needs to learn from worldwide best practices but apply them judiciously to meet its specific needs[7].

In the fast globalizing world, where countries are aiming at reducing import tariff barriers, India still has an ineffective indirect tax structure due to the cascading effect of multiple taxes on goods and services which affects cost of products and services. Further, increased complexity of taxation laws has led to high compliance cost and litigation. Few years back, two significant tax reforms were introduced by the Indian Government – Direct Tax Code and Goods and Service Tax. DTC aimed at placing the existing Income Tax Act, incorporated various provisions with the international taxation laws. Currently DTC is still undergoing changes and is yet to be tabled in parliament. The Indian Government has been trying to build consensus amongst political parties and states, for introducing Goods and Service Tax, which will allow government to regulate taxing on goods and services, rather than the current system of state regulations, but without much success. Both the new legislation, DTC and GST, were viewed by the industry leaders as a much more progressive law and a game changer giving enormous boost to revenue collection. However, the Indian Government has been unable to implement DTC and GST so far[8].

Changing Trends of Tax in India

The Government raises finance for its revenue and capital expenditures from tax revenue sources.

7 Tax system Reforms in India Challenges Ahead, See: www.cfo-connect.com/title_detail.asp?art_id=265&cat_id=8

8 Articles.economictimes.indiatimes.com>collection>Income Tax Act.

I) Tax Revenue:-

India has a well developed tax structure. Since 1991, India's tax structure and system has undergone several changes. Following are trends in tax revenue in India

1) Trends in Gross Tax Revenue and Tax GDP Ratio

Collection of direct and indirect taxes have increased due to reduction in tax rates, simplification of tax procedures and high rate of growth of GDP. Though total tax collection has increased but tax - GDP ratio has remained same. In comparison with developed countries India's GDP ratio is very low.

Trends in Gross Tax Revenue

Year	Tax Revenue	% of GDP
1990-91	57,576	10.1
2004-05	2,16,266	8.8
2009-10	4,59,444	7.02

Source:- Economic Survey 2010-11

2) Share of Direct and Indirect Taxes

Direct tax has largely increased due to increase in corporate income tax. The contribution of indirect taxes rose from 71% in 1960 to 83% in 1990-91. Since then there has been a decline in percentage contribution of indirect taxes.

Share of Direct and Indirect Taxes

(% Of Total Tax Revenue)

Year	Direct Taxes	Indirect Taxes
1990-91	19.1	80.9
2004-05	43.3	56.1
2009-10	58.6	39.5

Source:- Economic Survey 2010-11

3) Trends in Direct Taxes

Over the years the share of direct taxes has increased from 19% in

1990-91 to 58% in 2009-10. Direct tax rates have been declining since 1990-91.

Some of the major Direct taxes are:-

a) Corporate income Tax

Corporate Income Tax is the most important direct taxes in terms of revenue collection and contribution to total tax revenue. Since 1990-91 contribution of this tax to total tax revenue has increased due to growing corporate profits and after introduction of reforms.

Trends in Corporate Income Tax

Year	Rs. Crore	% of Total Tax Revenue
1990-91	5,335	9.3
2004-05	82,680	27.1
2009-10	2,44,630	39.0

Source:- Economic Survey 2010-11

b) Personal Income Tax

Personal Income tax is a progressive tax. Since 1990-91 collection of personal income tax has increased.

Trends in Personal Income Tax

Year	Rs. Crore	% of Total Tax Revenue
1990-91	5,371	9.3
2004-05	49,268	16.2
2009-10	1,22,280	19.5

Source:- Economic Survey 2010-11

4) Trends in Indirect Taxes

The burden of indirect taxes can be shifted from manufacturer to consumer. Government uses indirect taxes not only to raise revenue but also to achieve different socio - economic objectives like control of prices, maintaining sufficient supply of essential commodities and promote growth.

Some of the major Indirect taxes are:-

a) Customs Duty

Customs duty is indirect tax levied on goods imported into India as well as on goods exported from. The peak rate of customs duty at present is 10%.

Trends in Customs Duty

Year	Rs. Crore	% of Total Tax Revenue
1990-91	20,644	35.9
2004-05	57,611	18.9
2009-10	84,244	13.4

Source:- Economic Survey 2010-11

b) Excise Duty

Excise duty is levied on goods manufactured in India and meant for home consumption. Excise duty, is the biggest single source of revenue for Government. At present the peak excise duty is 10%. Since 1990-91, there has been a declining trend in excise duty.

Trends in Excise Duty

Year	Rs. Crore	% of Total Tax Revenue
1990-91	24,514	42.6
2004-05	99,125	32.5
2009-10	1,04,659	16.7

Source: - Economic Survey 2010-11

c) Service Tax

Service tax is levied services provided by certain categories of persons / firms / agencies. Since its inception in 1994, it has shown steady rise.

Trends in Service Tax

Year	Rs. Crore	% of Total Tax Revenue
1995-96	862	0.8

Year	Rs. Crore	% of Total Tax Revenue
2004-05	14,200	4.7
2009-10	58,454	9.3

Source:- Economic Survey 2010-11

Challenges and Suggestions

In Indian tax system, it is widely accepted that a significant portion of potential tax revenue is not collected because of poor tax administration and high tax evasion in India. The question is whether the complexity of tax structure or high tax rates have led to a high incidence of tax evasion, or if tax administration by itself has been unable to fulfill the revenue objectives implied by the tax structure. In practice it is likely that both tax policy and tax administration have mutually affected each other. It is imperative to identify the role of the tax administration, so that responsibility and accountability is clearly established. India is in a desperate need to reform its tax laws. For over two years, laws on the Goods and Service tax have been delayed, which will allow the Central Government to regulate taxes on services and certain goods, rather than the current system of state regulations. In the current system it is extremely difficult for business to run operations across the 28 states. The dramatic trends in India's economic evolution in recent years mainly point to the need to shed old assumptions and to take a fresh look at how best to design and implement India's tax policies .Lower statutory rates with base broadening could help achieve a pro-growth fiscal adjustment in India. There is the need to increase the scope for raising direct tax revenue through the removal of exemptions and improved tax administration. In addition to reducing tax induced distortions, the removal of exemptions would create room to further improve the neutrality of the economic reforms.

Foreign Investment Flows in India

Dr R K Kaundal*

Associate Professor

Govt.P.G. College,Dharamshala

Abstract

The present study takes an overview of the foreign investment flows in India since 1991. It also discusses the policy issues arising from foreign investment flows in India and important conclusions thereof. FDI is an important vehicle for the transfer of technology and knowledge and it demonstrates that it can have a long-term effect on growth by generating increasing returns in production via positive externalities and productive spillovers through channels such as imitation, competition, linkages, technology transfer, and training. The approvals of FDI inflows since the liberalisation of policy in 1991 reveal a dramatic jump. FDI and portfolio investments have steadily increased over the 1990s thus bringing down the relative reliance on external commercial borrowings and short-term credit. The average share of total investment in GDP which was 1.1 percent in 1991-92 to 2000-01 has increased to 2.20 percent during 2001-02 to 2012-13. FDI which constituted 96.99 percent of the total investment in 1991-92 has declined to 73.42 percent of the total investment in 2012-13. The share of the portfolio investment to total investment during the same period has increased from 3.01 percent to 26.58 percent. The establishment and strengthening of the FDI institutions such as Foreign Investment Promotion Board (FIPB), Secretariat of Industrial Assistance (SIA) and Foreign Investment Implementation Authority (FIIA) to facilitate FDI moving beyond approval to implementation has certainly helped attracting foreign investment.

I. Introduction

The basic philosophy underlying Indian economy during the post independent era of planning was rooted in mixed economy regime in which public sector with a view to achieve the overall growth of an economy on socialistic pattern of society. However the Indian economy grew at a low rate. This low growth was the result of the strategy of development which was, for the most part, and import-substitution industrialization strategy. Inadequate infrastructure and lack of experience stretched the gestation period and increased the costs. Indian economy faced serious crises of the nature macro-economic mismanagement, growing internal imbalance in fiscal situation and external imbalance in balance of payments situation. (Jalan, 1996).

All this provided an opportunity for a major reorientation of Indian economic policy. In July, 1991 the Government announced a series of economic reforms program, which included significant reduction in tariffs and elimination of import quotas except for consumer goods, elimination or reduction of restrictions on foreign ownership, current account convertibility on the trade account reduction in licensing requirements, regulations and red-tapism. It requires reduction of country's spending to the level parallel to its income and thereby reducing its fiscal deficit. The success of economic reforms depends on the country's involvement in the reforms programme (Kumar, 2000).

Thus to become, successful, it is quite essential that people's sentiment should go in favour of reforms. In order to provide greater scope to private sector, this new policy introduced various policy changes regarding industrial licensing, technology up-gradation, elimination of controls and restrictions, foreign equity capital, fiscal policy, rationalization and simplifying the system of fiscal and administrative regulation and export-import policy. These policy changes were brought with the sole intention to create a favourable climate for getting a big boost in private sector investment which would in turn usher in rapid growth of the economy as well as pave the way for modernisation of the economy (Dhar, 2012)

One of the remarkable features of globalisation since 1991 has been the flow of private capital in the form of foreign direct investment (FDI), which is an important source of development finance for developing countries, and which contributes to productivity gains by providing new investment, better technology, management expertise, and export markets. Given resource constraints and lack of investment in developing countries like India, market forces and the private sector are increasingly been relied on as the engines of economic growth (Abraham,1994). FDI promotes economic growth by increasing investment in its efficiency. FDI not only supplements domestic investment but also acts as a source of foreign exchange and ease pressure on the balance of payments (BoP). Considering the economic benefits of FDI, India has adopted wide ranging reforms since the early 1990s to attract FDI to ease the pressure on rising current account deficit (CAD), depreciating rupee, stagnating investment, and the slowdown of the growth rate (Prasana, 2008).

Against this background, this paper examines the impact of economic reforms on the external sector of India. The paper is structured as follow. Section I is introduction. Source of data and methodology is given in the Section II. Section III provides a brief contour of the FDI reforms in India, and Section IV presents the FDI trends in India. Conclusion and main findings are provided in the final section.

II. Data and Methodology

The present study is a modest attempt to take an overview of the foreign investment flow in India since 1991 along with the compound growth rates and instability indices. The present study is based upon the time series secondary data collected from various published sources of Govt. agencies. The data has been gathered from Economic Survey, Govt. of India, Ministry of Finance, New Delhi and Handbook of Statistics on India Economy, Reserve Bank of India, Mumbai. The value has been taken in the US dollars ($) as value in dollar terms is less volatile than the same measured in rupees.

Period of Analysis

To estimate the growth of foreign investment and its impact on the economy the study broadly covers the period of twenty two years from 1991-92 to 2012-13. This time period has been further divided into two sub periods Period-I (1991-92 to 2000-01) and Period-II (2001-02 to 2012-13).

Methodology and Techniques of Analysis

Estimation of Growth Rates

The compound growth rates have been calculated by using the following type of function.

$$Yi = a(bi)t$$

$$\text{Log} \quad Yi = \log a + t \log (bi)$$

where,

Yi = value of investment

t = time variable

Annual compound growth rate(r) was computed as:

$$r = [\text{anti} \log (bi)-1]* 100.$$

Measuring Instability

When certain economic activity show irregular changes during a year (apart from seasonal variations) or over a period of time that is considered as a form of economic instability (Lundberg, 1968). Coppock (1977) argued that instability means "excessive departure from some normal level".

As a measure of instability this analysis utilizes an exponential index (IXEXP). The equation of the exponential trend is written as: $X_{it} = a_i e^{bit} u_{it}$, Where (X_{it}) is the value, t represents time and u is the disturbance term. OLS is then used to estimate the equations. Export instability index IXEXP is defined as the standard deviation of the observed deviations from the estimated exponential time trend.

$$\text{Instability Index} = \left[\sum_{i=1}^{n} e_i^2 / n-k\right]^{\frac{1}{2}} \times 100 / \bar{X}$$

where $ei = [x_{it} - \alpha_i e^{\beta it}]$

This instability index has two advantages. First this is scale independent and can be used for cross comparisons. Secondly, it estimates the coefficient of variation, corrected for exponential trend, which is useful in policy decisions, on the long-term basis, as they are taken in terms of growth rates rather than in absolute increments.

III. FDI Reforms in India

Economic growth in any country depends upon the sustained growth of productive capacity, supported by savings and investment. FDI which brings new technology and knowledge along with capital is considered as a good substitute for debt in developing economies for higher investment and growth (Nagraj & Singh, 2008). FDI also incorporates new inputs and new varieties of intermediate goods in production. As the stock of physical capital increases its productive capacity and per capita output growth also increases. FDI may lead to increasing return to production via externalities and productivity spillovers through channels such as imitation, competition, linkages, technology transfer, and training (Sahoo, 2012a). Therefore FDI have a long term substantial and sustainable effect on the host country. The literature on FDI identifies four main channels of technological spillovers to the host country; (1) competition; (2) learning by doing; (3) labour skills; and (4) linkage.

Further FDI helps integrate the developing economies in to the global economy by easing access to foreign markets and including local enterprise in global production chain (Dua and Rasheed, 1998). FDI contributes to improving the host economy's export competitiveness and volume by (1) augmenting domestic capital for exports; (2) helping transfer of technology; (3) facilitating access to new and large foreign markets; and (4) providing training for the local workforce and upgrading technical and management skills.

FDI and Pre-Liberalization Period

India had followed an extremely cautious and selective approach while formulating FDI policy in view of the dominance of "import-substitution strategy" of industrialization. With the objective of becoming "self reliant", there was a dual nature of policy intention – FDI through foreign collaboration was welcomed in the areas of high technology and high priorities to build national capability and discouraged in low technology areas to protect and nurture domestic industries. The regulatory framework was consolidated through the enactment of Foreign Exchange Regulation Act (FERA) 1973 wherein foreign equity holding in a joint venture was allowed only up to 40 percent. Subsequently, various exemptions were extended to foreign companies engaged in export oriented businesses and high technology and high priority areas including allowing equity holdings of over 40 percent. Moreover, drawing from successes of other country experiences in Asia, Government not only established special economic zones (SEZs) but also designed liberal policy and provided incentives for promoting FDI in these zones with a view to promote exports. As India continued to be highly protective, these measures did not add substantially to export competitiveness (Nagraj, 2003). Recognizing these limitations, partial liberalization in the trade and investment policy was introduced in the 1980s with the objective of enhancing export competitiveness, modernisation and marketing of exports through Transnational Corporations (TNCs). The announcements of Industrial Policy (1980 and 1982) and Technology Policy (1983) provided for a liberal attitude towards foreign investments in terms of changes in policy directions. The policy was characterised by de-licensing of some of the industrial rules and promotion of Indian manufacturing exports as well as emphasising on modernisation of industries through liberalised imports of capital goods and technology. This was supported by trade liberalisation measures in the form of tariff reduction and shifting of large number of items from import licensing to Open General Licensing (OGL).

FDI and Post-Liberalisation Period

A major shift occurred when India embarked upon economic liberalization and reforms program in 1991 aiming to raise its growth potential and integrating with the world economy. Industrial policy reforms gradually removed restrictions on investment projects and business expansion on the one hand and allowed increased access to foreign technology and funding on the other. A series of measures that were directed towards liberalizing foreign investment included: (i) introduction of dual route of approval of FDI – RBI's automatic route and Government's approval (SIA/FIPB) route, (ii) automatic permission for technology agreements in high priority industries and removal of restriction of FDI in low technology areas as well as liberalisation of technology imports, (iii) permission to Non-resident Indians (NRIs) and Overseas Corporate Bodies (OCBs) to invest up to 100 percent in high priorities sectors, (iv) hike in the foreign equity participation limits to 51 percent for existing companies and liberalisation of the use of foreign "brands name" and (v) signing the convention of Multilateral Investment Guarantee Agency (MIGA) for protection of foreign investments (Kumar 2005). These efforts were boosted by the enactment of Foreign Exchange Management Act (FEMA), 1999 [that replaced the Foreign Exchange Regulation Act (FERA),

1973] which was less stringent. This along with the sequential financial sector reforms paved way for greater capital account liberalisation in India. Investment proposals falling under the automatic route and matters related to FEMA are dealt with by RBI, while the Government handles investment through approval route and issues that relate to FDI policy per se through its three institutions, viz., the Foreign Investment Promotion Board (FIPB), the Secretariat for Industrial Assistance (SIA) and the Foreign Investment Implementation Authority (FIIA).

FDI under the automatic route does not require any prior approval either by the Government or the Reserve Bank. The investors are only required to notify the concerned regional office of the RBI within 30 days of receipt of inward remittances and file the required documents with that office within 30 days of issuance of shares to foreign investors. Under the approval route, the proposals are considered in a time-bound and transparent manner by the FIPB. Approvals of composite proposals involving foreign investment/foreign technical collaboration are also granted on the recommendations of the FIPB. Current FDI policy in terms of sector specific limits has been summarised in Table 1.

Sector	FDI Cap/ Equity	Entry Route	Other Conditions
A. Agriculture			
1. Floriculture, Horticulture, Development of seeds, Animal Husbandry, Pisciculture, Aquaculture, cultivation of vegetables and mushrooms and services related to agro and allied sectors.	100%	Automatic	
2. Tea Sector, including plantation	100%	FIPB	

Sector	FDI Cap/ Equity	Entry Route	Other Conditions
B. Industry			
1. Mining covering exploration and mining of Diamonds and precious stones; gold, silver and minerals,	100%	Automatic	
2. Coal and lignite mining for captive consumption by power projects, and iron & steel, cement production.	100%	Automatic	
3. Mining and mineral separation of titanium bearing minerals	100%	FIPB	
C. Manufacturing			
1. Alcohol- Distillation & Brewing	100%	Automatic	
2. Coffee and Rubber processing & Warehousing	100%	Automatic	
3. Defence production	26%	FIPB	
4. Hazardous chemicals and isocyanates	100%	Automatic	
5. Industrial explosives-manufacture	100%	Automatic	
6. Drugs and Pharmaceuticals	100%	Automatic	
7. Power including generation (except Atomic Energy); Transmission, distribution and power trading.	100%	Automatic	
FDI is not permitted for generation, transmission & distribution of electricity produced in atomic power plant/atomic energy since private investment in this activity is prohibited and reserved for public sector.			
D. Services			
1. Civil aviation (Greenfield projects and existing projects)	100%	Automatic	
2. Asset Reconstruction Companies	49%	FIPB	

Sector	FDI Cap/ Equity	Entry Route	Other Conditions
3. Banking (Private) sector	74% (FDI+FII), FII not to exceed 49%	FIPB	
4. NBFCs: underwriting, portfolio management services, investment advisory services, financial consultancy, stock broking, asset management, venture capital, custodian, factoring, leasing and finance, housing finance, forex broking etc.	100%	Automatic	s.t. minimum capitalisation norms
5. Broadcasting			
a. FM radio	20%	FIPB	
b. Cable networking; c. Direct to home; d. Hardware facilities such as up-linking, HUB.	49% (FDI+FII)		
e. Up-linking a news and current affairs TV Channel	100%	FIPB	
6. Commodity Exchanges	49% (FDI+FII) (FDI 26% and FII 23%)		
7. Insurance	26%	Automatic	Clearance from IRDA
8. Petroleum and natural gas;			
a. Refining	49% (PSUs) 100% (private companies)	FIPB (for PSUs) Automatic (for private)	
9. Print Media			s.t. guidelines by Ministry of I & B
a. Publishing of newspaper and periodicals dealing with news and current affairs	26%	FIPB	
b. Publishing of scientific magazines/speciality journals/periodicals	100%	FIPB	
10. Telecommunications;			
a. Basic and cellular, unified access services, national/ international long distance, V-SAT, public mobile radio trunked services (PMRTS), global mobile personal communication services (GMPCS) and others.	74% (including FDI, FII, NRI, FCCBs, ADRs, GDRs, convertible preference shares, etc.	Automatic up to 49% and FIPB beyond 49%	

Sector where FDI is banned

1. Retail trading (Except single brand product retailing);
2. Atomic Energy
3. Lottery Business including Government/private lottery, online lotteries etc.;
4. Gambling and betting including casinos etc.;
5. Business of chit funds;
6. Nidhi Company;
7. Trading in Transferable Development Rights (TDRs);
8. Activities/sector not opened to private sector investment;
9. Agriculture (excluding floriculture, horticulture, development of seeds, animal husbandry, pisciculture and cultivation of vegetables, mushrooms etc. under controlled conditions and services related to agro and allied sectors) and plantations (other than tea plantations);
10. Real estate business, or construction of farm houses;
11. Manufacturing of cigars, cheroots, cigarillos and cigarettes, of tobacco or of tobacco substitutes.

Source:- Compiled from the various published sources of government agencies.

IV. FDI Trends in India

Foreign Direct Investment inflow into India is assumed to play a vital role as a source of capital, management and technology. It implies that FDI can have positive effects on a host economy's development efforts. Many countries like India have offered incentives to encourage FDI to their economies. FDI have a favourable short-term effect on growth as it expands the economic activity. However, in the long run it reduces the growth rate due to dependency, particularly due to "Recapitalization". This is due to the reason that the foreign investors repatriate their investment by contracting the economic activities in the long-run. FDI is an important vehicle for the transfer of technology and knowledge and it demonstrates that it can have a long-run effect on growth by generating increasing returns in production via positive externalities and productive spillovers. Further the level of capital is crucial for a country to benefit from technology spillovers of MNE's. Increasing industrialization of production led by globalization and liberalization has been contributing for increasing foreign direct investment (FDI) inflows across countries in the world. FDI inflows can lead to several economic and welfare implications for host country. FDI inflows, which come as a composite bundle of tangible and intangible assets, can augment of resources (e.g., raising productivity) expending market (e.g., increasing exports). This composite bundle of tangible and intangible assets, among others, comprises transfer of state of the art technology, managerial expertise, access to world market and other firm specific intangible assets, among others, comprises transfer of state of the art technology, managerial expertise, access tó world market and other firm specific intangible assets. Transfer of these tangible and intangible assets are viewed as main factors behind the FDI induced growth in the host country. Thus FDI is an important determinant of output, employment and income of a host country (Sahoo, 2005). FDI has contributed significantly to GDP and productivity growth. The contribution of FDI to annual GDP growth through capital deepening was on an arrange 0.4 percent in the 1990s and the contribution to long term total factor productivity growth on an average was 25 percent over the same period. Hence the total contribution of FDI to GDP growth during the 1990s was estimated at about 3 percent a year. This positive link between FDI and GDP has been found at both national and provincial levels.

The approvals of FDI inflows since the liberalization of policy in 1991 reveal a dramatic jump. Liberalisation of foreign investment policy regime was an important aspect of the reforms. The approvals of FDI inflows since the liberalisation of policy in 1991 reveal a dramatic jump. FDI and portfolio investments have steadily increased over the 1990s thus bringing down the relative reliance on external commercial borrowings and short-term credit. Compared to total FDI totalling US$ 129 million in 1991-92, US$ 3557 million worth of FDI inflows have been approved in the year 1997-98, rose to US$ 34298 million in the year 2012-13. The average share of total investment in GDP which was 1.1 percent in 1991-92 to 2000-01 has increased to 2.20 percent during 2001-02 to 2012-13. FDI which constituted 96.99 percent of the total investment in 1991-92 has declined to 73.42 percent of the total investment in 2012-13. The share of the portfolio investment to total investment during the same period has increased from 3.01 percent to 26.58 percent. The share of total investment to GDP which was 0.05 percent in 1991-92 has increased to highest level of 3.77 percent in 2009-10 and the declined to 2.57 percent in 2012-13 (Table 2).

Year	A. Direct investment		B. Portfolio investment		(A+B). Total Investment		% of GDP
	Rs. Crore	US $ million	Rs. Crore	US $ million	Rs. Crore	US $ million	
1991-92	316	129	10	4	326	133	0.05
1992-93	965	315	748	244	1713	559	0.22
1993-94	1838	586	11188	3567	13026	4153	1.53
1994-95	4126	1314	12007	3824	16133	5138	1.61
1995-96	7172	2144	9192	2748	16364	4892	1.40
1996-97	10015	2821	11758	3312	21773	6133	1.61
1997-98	13220	3557	6794	1828	20014	5385	1.33
1998-99	10358	2462	-257	-61	10101	2401	0.59
1999-00	9338	2155	13112	3026	22450	5181	1.16
2000-01	18406	4029	12609	2760	31015	6789	1.50
2001-02	29235	4095	9639	2021	38874	8151	1.74
2002-03	24367	2764	4738	979	29105	6014	1.29
2003-04	19860	2229	52279	11377	72139	15699	2.70
2004-05	27188	6051	41854	9291	69042	13003	1.88
2005-06	39674	9697	55307	12492	94981	16261	2.05
2006-07	103367	22826	31713	6947	135080	14640	1.57
2007-08	140180	34843	109741	27434	249921	43325	3.56
2008-09	161536	41873	-63618	-14032	97918	8311	0.69

Year	A. Direct investment		B. Portfolio investment		(A+B). Total Investment		% of GDP
	Rs. Crore	US $ million	Rs. Crore	US $ million	Rs. Crore	US $ million	
2009-10	176304	37745	153511	32396	329815	50361	3.77
2010-11	159320	34847	138495	30292	190181	41597	2.48
2011-12	217263	46553	80137	17171	182839	39177	2.11
2012-13	183254	34298	143678	26891	249572	46710	2.57

Source: Reserve Bank of India (Mumbai), Handbook of Statistics on Indian Economy.

Table 3: Equity FDI inflows to India

Sectors	2006-07	2007-08	2008-09	2009-10	2010-11
Sectoral Shares (percent)					
Manufactures	17.6	19.2	21.0	22.9	32.1
Services	56.9	41.2	45.1	32.8	30.1
Construction, Real estate and mining	15.5	22.4	18.6	26.6	17.6
Others	9.9	17.2	15.2	17.7	20.1
Total	100.0	100.0	100.0	100.0	100.0
Equity Inflows (US$ billions)					
Manufactures	1.6	3.7	4.8	5.1	4.8
Services	5.3	8.0	10.2	7.4	4.5
Construction, Real Estate and mining	1.4	4.3	4.2	6.0	2.6
Others	0.9	3.3	3.4	4.0	3.0
Total Equity FDI	9.3	19.4	22.7	22.5	14.9

Source:- Reserve Bank of India (Mumbai), Handbook of Statistics on Indian Economy.

From a sectoral perspective, FDI in India mainly flowed into services sector with an average share of 41 percent in the past five years followed by manufacturing around 23 percent. However, the share of services declined over the years from almost 57 percent in 2006-07 to about 30 percent in 2010-11, while the shares of manufacturing and others largely comprising electricity and other power generation increased over the same period (Table 3). Sectoral information on the recent trends in FDI flows to India show that the moderation in gross equity FDI flows during 2010-11 has been mainly driven by sectors such as construction, real estate and mining and services such as business and financial services. Manufacturing, which has been the largest recipient of FDI in India, has also witnessed some moderation (Table 3).

Measurement of Compound Growth Rate and Instability of Foreign Investment Flow in India

While the magnitude of inflows has recorded impressive growth, they are still at small levels compared to the country's potential. Furthermore, one of the objectives of the current reforms of policies is to remove the impediments for export-oriented manufacture in general and to attract MNEs to locate efficiency-seeking FDI in the country (Sharma, 2000). These investments could help in expanding, manufactured exports by using her as an export platform. The majority of the approvals of the FDI in the recent years aim to exploit India's sizeable and expanding domestic market. The efficiency seeking or export-oriented FDI have yet to start flowing to the country in a considerable manner.

Table 4: Compound Growth Rates and Instability of the Major Indicators of the External Sector.

(Value in US$ million)

Indicators/Years	1991-92 to 2000-01		2001-02 to 2012-13	
	G	I	G	I
Total Exports (X)	10.14	0.90	20.10	0.83
Total Imports (M)	11.87	0.78	24.01	1.13
Foreign Exchange Reserves	17.38	1.93	16.23	2.05
Foreign Total Investment	34.35	12.41	22.62	3.72
Foreign Direct Investment	39.45	8.04	33.20	5.61
Foreign Portfolio Investment	38.78	33.19	16.02	32.49

Indicators/Years	1991-92 to 2000-01		2001-02 to 2012-13	
	G	I	G	I
Total Debt	1.51	0.29	13.08	0.71
Short Term Debt	-5.66	2.76	38.54	3.65
Long Term Debt	2.05	0.42	10.45	0.69

G-Compound growth rate. I- Instability.

Source: Reserve Bank of India (Mumbai), Handbook of Statistics on Indian Economy.

International capital flow such as direct and portfolio has a huge contribution to influence the economic behaviour of the countries positively. Foreign Investment may be determined by the factors, which operate either through technology and managerial skills, or the work culture and the synergies accompanying capital flows that seem to give a lot more contribution to growth (Damija, 2008). Even with regard to portfolio flow from foreign institutional investors the way in which FIIs assess market practices in stock exchanges have enhanced our own practice and skill among participants to global standards (Chakrabarti, 2001). Table 4 presents the estimated annual compound growth rates of total foreign investment, foreign direct investment, foreign portfolio investment, foreign exchange reserves, total debt, short-term debt and long-term debt for the period 1991-92 to 2000-01 and 2001-02 to 2012-13. The growth rate of total exports, total imports, total debt, short term and long term debt has increased during 2001-02 to 2012-13 over 1991-92 to 2000-01. Whereas growth rate for foreign exchange reserves, foreign total investment, foreign direct investment, and foreign portfolio investment has declined during the same period. Instability for total exports, foreign total investment, foreign direct investment, and foreign portfolio investment has declined and for total imports, foreign exchange reserves, total debt, short term debt and long term debt has increased during the study period.

V. Conclusions, Challenges and Main Findings

Recent FDI Reforms

Reforms that are essential to sustain and increase FDI into India include the following. Relaxation of ceilings for foreign equity in many sectors such as civilian goods or dual use equipment used in the production of civilian goods, public sector refineries and oil marketing, banking, small scale industry, power generation etc. Similarly the equity limit for FDI should be raised to 100 percent from 49 percent for investment companies. India could attract a huge amount of FDI in real estate, provided the plethora of controls was removed and rules and regulations were properly designed, and clear. Any early decision on allowing 51 percent FDI in e-commerce would be useful. The Government at present permits 100 percent FDI in only business-to business (B2B) e-commerce transactions in goods. Putting more and more sectors under automatic route is certainly useful for more FDI realisation (Sahoo, 2012).

Challenges and Unfinished Agenda

Though FDI inflows to India have increased over last two decades, India still lags behind countries like China, Singapore, or Brazil. FDI inflows to India are still concentrated in a few sectors and a few states because of unresolved issues and India is yet to receive FDI inflows to its full potential. Besides all these advantages India has, there are still factors and issues that hinder FDI flow into India including; (i) infrastructure bottlenecks, (ii) rigid and complicated labour laws, (iii) lack of coordination between centre and states, (iv) FDI caps/ceilings in many sectors where 100 percent FDI equity is not allowed for feasible investment projects, and (v) difficult bureaucratic controls and procedures to get the necessary clearances and approvals.

Findings

The approvals of FDI inflows since the liberalization of policy in

1991 reveal a dramatic jump. Liberalisation of foreign investment policy regime was an important aspect of the reforms. The approvals of FDI inflows since the liberalisation of policy in 1991 reveal a dramatic jump. FDI and portfolio investments have steadily increased over the 1990s thus bringing down the relative reliance on external commercial borrowings and short-term credit. Compared to total FDI totalling US$ 129 million in 1991-92, US$ 3557 million worth of FDI inflows have been approved in the year 1997-98, rose to US$ 34298 million in the year 2012-13. The average share of total investment in GDP which was 1.1 percent in 1991-92 to 2000-01 has increased to 2.20 percent during 2001-02 to 2012-13. FDI which constituted 96.99 percent of the total investment in 1991-92 has declined to 73.42 percent of the total investment in 2012-13. The share of the portfolio investment to total investment during the same period has increased from 3.01 percent to 26.58 percent. The share of total investment to GDP which was 0.05 percent in 1991-92 has increased to highest level of 3.77 percent in 2009-10 and the declined to 2.57 percent in 2012-13

From a sectoral perspective, FDI in India mainly flowed into services sector with an average share of 41 percent in the past five years followed by manufacturing around 23 percent. However, the share of services declined over the years from almost 57 percent in 2006-07 to about 30 percent in 2010-11, while the shares of manufacturing and others largely comprising electricity and other power generation increased over the same period. Sectoral information on the recent trends in FDI flows to India show that the moderation in gross equity FDI flows during 2010-11 has been mainly driven by sectors such as construction, real estate and mining and services such as business and financial services. Manufacturing, which has been the largest recipient of FDI in India, has also witnessed some moderation

The establishment and strengthening of the FDI institutions such as Foreign Investment Promotion Board (FIPB), Secretariat of Industrial Assistance (SIA) and Foreign Investment

Implementation Authority (FIIA) to facilitate FDI moving beyond approval to implementation has certainly helped in attracting investment in India.

Bibliography

Abraham, Joseph (1994), Boosting flow of Foreign Private Investment", Yojana, Vol. 38, No. 19.

Coppock, J. D, 1977), International Trade Instability. Farnborough: Saxon House, Teak field Ltd.

Chakrabarti, Rajesh (2001), "FII flows to India, Nature and Causes" Money and Finance, Vol. 2. Issue 7. Oct.-Dec.

Dhar, P.K. (2012), Indian Economy, its Growing Dimensions, Published by Usha Raj Kumar for Kalyani Publishers.

Damija, Nidi (2008), "Foreign Institutional Investment in India", The Journal of Applied Economic Research, Vol. 2, No. 3, pp. 287-320.

Government of India (2006), Foreign Direct Investment Policy, Ministry of Commerce and Industry, Department of Industrial Policy and Promotion, New Delhi.

Government of India (2007), FDI Statistics, Ministry of Commerce and Industrial, Department of Industrial Policy and Promotion, New Delhi.

Government of India, Economic Survey, Controller of Publication, New Delhi (various issues).

Sharma, K. (2000), "Export Growth in India: Has FDI Played a Role?" Discussion papers 816, Yale University, Economic Growth Center, New Haven, Conn., mimeo.

Jalan, Bimal (1996), India's Economic Policy, preparing for the twenty first century, Vikas, New Delhi.

Lundberg, Eric (1968), Instability and Economic Growth, New Haven: Yale University Press.

Nagraj, R. (2003), "Foreign Direct Investment in India in the 1990s Trend and Issues", Economic and Political weekly, Vol. 38, No. 17 pp. 1701-12.

Nagraj, Komal and Ravi Inder Singh (2008), "Position of Foreign Direct Investment in India", the ICFAI university, Journal of Financial Economics, Vol. VI, No. 3, pp. 84-92.

Prasanna, P.K. (2008), "Foreign Institutional Investors: Investment Preference in India", JOAAG, Vol. 3, No. 2.

Kumar, Nagesh (2000) "Economic Reforms and Their Macro Economic Impact", Economic and Political Weekly, 35(10): pp. 803-812.

---------------------- (2005), "Liberalization, Foreign Direct Investment Flows and Development, Indian Experience in the 1990s, Economic and Political Weekly, pp. 459-469 (April).

Patel, Mitesh and Ritesh Patel (2012), "A Study on FDI and Economic Growth in Selected Association: Evidence from Granger Casuality Test", Int. J. Eco. Res. 3(5), pp. 119-128.

Reserve Bank of India (2012), Handbook of Statistic on Indian Economy, Mumbai.

Sahoo, P. (2012a), "Foreign Direct Investment in India: Unfinished Agenda", 'Economic Reform Processes in South Asia: Towards Policy Efficiency' ed. Philippa Dee, Routledge, pp. 109-136, Australlia.

-------------(2013), "FDI Reforms in India: Steps in the Right Direction", Yojana, December Vol. 57, pp. 38-43.

Sirari, Arjun Singh and Narender Singh Bohra (2011), "Foreign Direct Investment in India Service Sector: A Study of Post Liberalization", Int. J. Eco. Res. 2(2), pp. 10-18.

Globalization As A Part of Economic Reforms: A Journey Started

Dr. Raj Kumar Sandal (Associate Professor)
Govt. P.G. College Amb
Ph. 09418465173
Email :- sandal8923@gmail.com

Abstract

Economic reforms consist of three aspects, i.e. Liberalization, Privatization and Globalization (L.P.G.). Out of three Ist two are related to the domestic resources, rules and policies, where as the third one (Globalization) is the aspect which is having global impact.Globalization is the process of integrating various economies of the world without creating any obstacles and barriers in the flow of goods and services. The process of globalization deals with reduction of trade barriers, free flow of capital, free flow of technology and creation of environment in which free flow of labour can take place in different countries of the world. The advocates of the policy of globalization argue that the globalization would help the under-developed countries to improve their competitive strength to attain higher growth rates. On these lines various countries of the world have adopted the policy of globalization. Following the same path India has adopted the same policy since 1991 and started the process of dismantling trade barriers along with abolishing quantitative restrictions (QRs) phase wise. Accordingly the govt. of India has been reducing the peak rates of custom duty in subsequent budgets and removing quantitative restrictions on the remaining items in the EXIM policy 2001-2002. All these have resulted in open access to new markets and new technology for the country. Evaluating the process of globalization and new economic policy of Govt. of India (June 1991), this paper is an attempt to study the impact of globalization on imports-exports, labor market, flow of market, transfer of technology, employment and poverty in India.

Globalization and its Impact on India

The claims of the protagonists of globalization have been examined by various researches in different countries. A very powerful critique of globalization has been made by Stiglitz, Nobel Prize winner for Economics (2001) and former Chief Economist of the World Bank. The World Commission on the Social Dimension of Globalization (WCSDG) set up by ILO has also considered the experience of globalization the world over and made certain very revealing observations. The world commission states :" The current path of globalization must change. Too few share in its benefits. Too many have no voice in its design and no influence on its course". "We wish to make globalization a means to expand human well-being and freedom, and to bring democracy and development to local communities where people live.

Foreign Investment Flows

It is often claimed that globalization leads to a greater flow of foreign investment, which should help to increase the productive capacity of the recipient economy. Foreign investment takes two forms- foreign direct investment (FDI) and foreign portfolio investment (FPI). Foreign direct investment helps to increase the productive capacity of the economy, while foreign portfolio investment is of a more speculative nature and is thus very volatile. A careful perusal of the data on foreign investment reveals that during the period 1990-91 and 1994-95, the share of FDI in total investment inflow was only 24.2 percent and that of FPI was 75.8 percent. In other words, only a quarter of the total foreign investment was available for increasing productive capacity while about three quarters was very volatile. For the 5-year period (1995-96 to 2000), the proportion of FDI in total foreign investment improved to 54.8 percent. However, the share of FPI was still high at about 45 percent. During the next 10 year period (2000-01 to 2010-11), the share of FDI was 60.8 percent and that of FPI was 39.2 percent. Compared with this situation, the data about FDI shows a gradual upwards growth from $129 million in 1991-92 to $1,314 million in 1994-95, to further rise to $3,557 million in 1997-98. Subsequently we find increase in FDI in leaps and bounds to $37,763 million by 2009-10. During 2010-11, their was a decline in FDI in flow to $ 24024 million. It implies that as a matter of policy, the host country can depend on a regular inflow of FDI if it creates a conducive climate for the purpose.

Fall in employment growth rates

Globalization has resulted in a fall in the employment growth rates. The annual growth rate of employment which was 2.04 percent during 1983-94, the same rate declined to a mere 0.98 percent during the period 1994-2000. As a result, the unemployment growth rates increased from 5.99 percent in 1993-94 to 7.32 percent in 1990-2000. This was despite the fall in the growth rate of labour force from 2.43 percent during 1983-1984 to 1.31 percent during 1993-2000. Such a situation is mostly resulted from the declaration in employment growth rates in agriculture and community and personal services. These two sectors contributed jointly around 70 percent of total employment generated but they virtually failed to record any growth in employment.

Thus after making a review of performance of the economy for a decade after the introduction of globalization, it is observed that the policy of globalization has not been able to bring the required benefits to the people in general in terms of basic macro indicators such as GDP growth rates, employment generation, reduction of poverty, hike in investment, boost in merchandise exports. It is only in respect of services export India has been able to record marginal gain due to its cheaper manpower resources.

Moreover as a result of globalization, a good number of small and medium scale enterprise had to face closure due to unequal competition leading to loss of employment to a good number of workers engaged in these industrial units. World commission on Social Dimension of Globalization (2004) unambiguously observed, " The goal of full employment and achieving decent work for all receives low priority in current international policies."..”There is no point to a globalization that reduces the price of child's shoes but costs the father his job." Thus globalization has also failed to look fairly at the small enterprises, rural and informal sectors from where majority of people earn their live hood. Thus under the present scenario, important steps need to be taken for integrating the growth objective with that of employment objective.

Inequality and Poverty

ILO Report (2004) in a very forthright manner states:" Income inequality has increased in some industrialized countries, reflected in an increase in the share of capital in national income as well as an increase in wage inequality between mid-1980s and the mid-1990s". In United States, the chief flag bearer of globalization, the share of top 1 percent of income earners reached 17 percent of gross income in 2000, a level last observed in the 1920s. This increased concentration of wealth has been the prime factor in the rise of inequality. Consequently, the share of the bottom 10 percent of wage earners has declined.

The widening inequality has been the result of the very high compensation (salaries and perks) paid by MNEs, the development of new business with a global reach and global "superstardoms". The public perception is that globalization has resulted in high degree of concentration of wealth.

The ILO Report (2004) identifying the people who have benefited most states:" As in the case of countries, the people who benefited most from globalization include those associated(as shareholders, managers, workers or sub-contractors) with successful MNEs and with internationally competitive national enterprise. More generally, those endowed with capital and other assets, entrepreneurial ability and education and skills are in increasing demand have all benefited".

"Conversely, the adversely affected include those associated with uncompetitive enterprises that have been unable to survive in the face of trade liberalization or the entry of foreign firms. These enterprises included those previously highly protected by trade barriers, subsidized state enterprise, and small and medium sized enterprise that had a limited capacity to adjust to a rapid liberalization of the economy".

Cheap imports lead to the closure of a large number of vulnerable small enterprises, they have adversely affected the informal economy as well as agriculture. The upshot is that as a consequence of globalization, the poor, the assestless and unskilled workers were the looser, and the rich endowed with capital and human capabilities have been the winners. This is particularly true of employment in firms acting as sub-contractors to Multinational Corporations (MNCs) even in labour intensive industries such as garments and footwear. To protect fundamental rights of the workers international action is necessary.

Increase of Imports Far Greater Than Increase of Exports

Globalizers advocated the acceptance of the new strategy of liberalization and globalization on the plea that India will be able to access foreign markets more effectively. Exports rose from 5.8 percent of GDP in 1990-91 to 9.1 percent of GDP in 1995-96. Thereafter we find a gradual increase in exports to reach 14.4 percent of GDP in 2009-10. But if we examine the trend of imports, they increased from 8.8 percent of GDP in 1990-91 to 23.1 percent in 2009-10. Even when exports fell in 1996-97 and 1997-98, imports continued their forward march. During 2000-01, when exports increased to level of 9.9 percent of GDP, imports jumped to a level of 12.6 percent of GDP. As a consequence, India's trade deficit during 1996-97 to 2000-01 ranged between 3.1 to 4.0 percent of GDP. The situation has slightly improved during 2001-02 and 2002-03 and the trade deficit has come down to 2.4 percent and 2.1 percent of GDP respectively. However, the situation again deteriorated in 2008-09 and trade deficit sharply increased to 9.7 percent of GDP. But in 2009-10, it was 8.7 percent of GDP.

This underlines the hard reality that foreigners have been able to penetrate the Indian market more effectively than Indians have been able to access foreign markets.

However, India's performance in achieving a net positive balance in invisible has helped it to wipe out the large trade deficit. During 2003-04, net invisibles showed a positive balance of 4.6 percent of GDP which not only wiped out the trade balance deficit, but created a positive balance in current account to the extent of 2.3 percent of GDP. A major contributor to the present situation is a massive inflow of foreign exchange from the software service provided by India as a consequence of sharp increase in exports of IT-enabled and business process outsourcing (BPO) services. However, the situation deteriorated since 2004-05 and a negative balance on current account appeared which continued and in 2009-10, negative BOP on current account was 3.1 percent of GDP.

Impact of Globalization on Agriculture Sector

Agricultural Sector is the mainstay of the rural Indian economy around which socio-economic privileges and deprivations revolve and any change in its structure is likely to have a corresponding impact on the existing pattern of Social equity. The liberalization of India's economy was adopted by India in 1991. Facing a severe economic crisis, India approached the IMF for a loan, and the IMF granted what is called a 'structural adjustment' loan, which is a loan with certain conditions attached which relate to a structural change in the economy. Essentially, the reforms sought to gradually phase out government control of the market (liberalization), privatize public sector organizations (privatization), and reduce export subsidies and import barriers to enable free trade (globalization). Globalization has helped in:

- Raising living standards,
- Alleviating poverty,
- Assuring food security,
- Generating buoyant market for expansion of industry and services, and
- Making substantial contribution to the national economic growth.

Impact of Globalization on Industrial Sector

Effects of Globalization on Indian Industry started when the government opened the country's markets to foreign investments in the early 1990s. Globalization of the Indian Industry took place in its various sectors such as steel, pharmaceutical, petroleum, chemical, textile, cement, retail, and BPO.

Globalization means the dismantling of trade barriers between nations and the integration of the nations economies through financial flow, trade in goods and services, and corporate investments between nations. Globalization has increased across the world in recent years due to the fast progress that has been made in the field of technology especially in communications and transport. The government of India made changes in its economic policy in 1991 by which it allowed direct foreign investments in the country. The benefits of the effects of globalization in the

Indian Industry are that many foreign companies set up industries in India, especially in the pharmaceutical, BPO, petroleum, manufacturing, and chemical sectors and this helped to provide employment to many people in the country. This helped reduce the level of unemployment and poverty in the country. Also the benefit of the Effects of Globalization on Indian Industry are that the foreign companies brought in highly advanced technology with them and this helped to make the Indian Industry more technologically advanced.

The negative Effects of Globalization on Indian Industry are that with the coming of technology the number of labour required decreased and this resulted in many people being removed from their jobs. This happened mainly in the pharmaceutical, chemical, manufacturing, and cement industries.

Social Services

About the quality of education given to children, the Approach to the Eleventh Five Year Plan stated: A recent study has found that 38 percent of the children who have completed four years of schooling cannot read a small paragraph with short sentences meant to be read by a student of Class II. About 55 percent of such children cannot divide a three digit number by a one digit number. These are indicators of serious learning problems which must be addressed.

The Approach paper added further: Universalisation of education will not suffice in the knowledge economy. A person with a mere eight years of schooling will be as disadvantaged in a knowledge economy by ICT as an illiterate person in modern industry an services.

The less said about the achievements in health the better. The Approach to the Eleventh Plan concedes that progress implementing the objectives of health have been slow. The Report gave the particulars of the rates of infant mortality (per 1000 live births) for India as 60 against Sri Lanka (13), China (30) and Vietnam (19). The rate of maternal mortality (per 1,

00,000 deliveries) of India is 407 against Sri Lanka (92), China (56) and Vietnam (130).

Growth of Unemployment Poverty

The proportion of the unemployed to the total labor force has been increasing from 2.62 percent (1993-94) to 2.78 percent (1999-2000) and 3.06 percent (2004-05). In absolute figures, the number of unemployed had been in those years 9.02 million, 10.51 million and 13.10 million respectively. (Economic Survey 2006-07, Table 10.4)

In reply to a question, the Minister for Labor and Employment informed the Lok Sabha on March 19, 2007, that the enrolment of the unemployed in the Employment Exchanges in 2006-07 was 79 lakhs against the average of 58 lakhs in the past ten years.

About the impact of globalization, in particular on the development of India, the ILO Report (2004) stated: In India, there had been winners and losers. The lives of the educated and the rich had been enriched by globalization. The information technology (IT) sector was a particular beneficiary. But the benefits had not yet reached the majority, and new risks had cropped up for the losersthe socially deprived and the rural poor. Significant numbers of non-perennial poor, who had worked hard to escape poverty, were finding their gains reversed. Power was shifting from elected local institutions to unaccountable trans-national bodies. Western perceptions, which dominated the globe media, were not aligned with local perspectives; they encouraged consumerism in the midst of extreme poverty and posed a threat to cultural and linguistic diversity.

Conclusion

Outlining the objectives of globalization, ILO report states," Our primary concerns are that globalization should benefit all countries and should raise the welfare of all people throughout the world". This implies that it should raise the rate of economic growth in poor countries and reduce world poverty, and that it should not increase inequalities or undermine socio-economic security within countries". (WCSDG- 2004 P 35). In that sense the world should move towards more "Humane Globalization". Mahatma Gandhi put it very simply:" There is enough in the world for everybody' needs, but there can not be enough for everybody's greed".However, globalization has not worked for the interest of the world's poor. It has led to increase in inequalities across the countries as well as with in the countries. It is not working to sustain environment. Thus if every thing moves in the same direction the fate of globalization will be under threat. Therefore all countries must strive for good political governance an democratic political system, an effective state which raises the capabilities of people trough universal access to education, social services and promote greater equality, a vibrant civil society empowered by freedom of association and expression and strong representative organizations of workers and employees which can share the fruits of globalization.

Last but not the least it is safe to conclude that the fault does not lie in globalization, but the way it has been managed.

References

1. Bhagwti, Jagdish (2004) " In defense of globalization" . Oxford University parse –New Dehli
2. Deoton, Angus and Dreze, Jean (2002) "Poverty and inequality in India". A re-examination" E.P.W. vol 37 No-45
3. Dhar, P.N. Economic reforms " Why we need them" -1992
4. Dreze and Sen Amarty (1995) India: Economic Development and social opportunity.
5. Dutt Rudder (1997) " Economic Reform in India"- A critique S.Chand & Company. New Dehli
6. Govt. of India "Economic survey: 2010-2011 and 2011-2012
7. ILO(2004) " A fair globalization : creating opportunities for all" Report of the world commission on the social dimension of globalization Geneva.
8. Mohat S.R. (2001) Reinvesting in Public Sector

9. Nayyar Deepak "India's export and import policies" (IPH) New Dehli
10. R.B.I. report on currency and finance 2001-2010
11. Scope (2001) Performance of Public & Private sector.
12. Singh Manmohan, "India's export trend (Oxford University press Londan)
13. Stiglitz Joseph E. 2002 , "Employment social institution and social well being" international labour review vol. 141 No-1-2
14. Tidsell Clem and Sen Raj Kumar(eds) 2004 " Economic Globalization" Edward Elgar (U.K.)
15. WCSDC-2004 (a report)
16. World Development Report – 2011-12

Performance of Indian Economy during Eleventh Five Year Plan

Seema Chandel

Assistant Professor,

Department – Sri Sai School of Management and

Commerce studies, Palampur. Distt-Kangra (H.P)

Abstract

India is today one of the sixth fastest growing economies of the world. Indian Economy is the ninth-largest in the world by nominal GDP and the third-largest by purchasing power parity. On a per-capita-income basis, India ranked 141st by nominal GDP and 130th by GDP (PPP) in 2012, according to the IMF. India is the 19th-largest exporter and the 10th-largest importer in the world. India's economic growth began slowing in 2011 because of a tight monetary policy, intended to address persistent inflation, and a decline in investment. The present paper deals with the study of some variables which are responsible for growth of Economy. The period of study is from 2007-12 and based on secondary information. The aim of this paper is to study about the growth rate at current market price, per capita income, and production of food grain, inflation, export and import of Indian Economy. In consonance to the objectives of study, the secondary data has been collected from Economic Survey (2012-13) and from the related websites. The tabulated data as per the requirements of the objectives of the study has been analyzed with appropriate methodology. The main findings of the study are the growth rate of Indian GDP has been fluctuating from last five yrs., per capita income of India has been increasing. There is an increase in the production in food grains in India from 2007-08 to 2011-12 except 2009-10, Inflation has been increasing from 2007-10, but decreasing in 2011, there is an increase in export from 2007-12 but import has been fluctuating from 2007-12.

Keywords: Growth Rate, Inflation, Export, Import, Production, GDP (Gross Domestic Product), PPP (Purchasing Power Parity), Income and Economy.

Introduction

Indian Economy is an underdeveloped and mixed economy. It is divided into three sectors: Primary, Secondary and Tertiary. Primary sector includes agriculture, forestry, dairy, etc and it contributes 14.1% in GDP, Secondary sector includes manufacturing, construction, power generation etc. and it contributes 26.9% in GDP and Tertiary sector includes services like banking, insurance, telecommunication etc and it contributes 59% in GDP. Indian Economy is the ninth-largest in the world by nominal GDP and the third-largest by purchasing power parity (PPP). On a per-capita-income basis, India ranked 141st by nominal GDP and 130th by GDP (PPP) in 2012, according to the IMF. India is the 19th-largest exporter and the 10th-largest importer in the world. The economy slowed to around 5.0% for the 2012–13 fiscal year compared with 6.2% in the previous fiscal.

The independence-era of Indian economy (from 1947 to 1991) was based on a mixed economy combining features of capitalism and socialism, resulting in an inward-looking, interventionist policies and import-substituting economy that failed to take advantage of the post-war expansion of trade. This model contributed to widespread inefficiencies and corruption, and the failings of this system were due largely to its poor implementation.

In 1991, India adopted liberal and free-market principles and liberalized its economy to international trade under the guidance of former Finance minister Manmohan Singh under the Prime Ministry of P.V. Narasimha Rao, who had eliminated License Raj, a pre- and post-British era mechanism of strict government controls on setting up new industry. Following these major economic reforms and a strong focus on developing national infrastructure such as the Golden Quadrilateral project by Atal Bihari Vajpayee, prime minister, the country's economic growth progressed at a rapid pace, with relatively large increases in per-capita incomes.

Review of Literature

According to a recent Goldman Sachs report, " Over the next fifty years, Brazil, India, Russia and China- the BRIC economies, could become a big larger force in the world economy" and India could emerge as the world's 3rd largest economy over the next four decades.

Objectives of Study

The paper is attempted with main objectives to study about the growth rate, per capita income, and production of food grain, inflation, export and import of Indian economy.

Importance of Study

Indian economy has been witnessing a phenomenal growth since the last decade but economic growth began slowing in 2011 because of a tight monetary policy, intended to address persistent inflation, and a decline in investment. Growth rate, Per Capita Income, Production, Inflation, Export and Import are important variables which are responsible for growth of Economy. Therefore it is important to study these variables.

Research Methodology

The data for the present study has been used from secondary sources. In consonance to the objectives of study, the secondary data has been collected from Economic Survey (2012-13) and from the related websites. The tabulated data as per the requirements of the objectives of the study has been analyzed with appropriate methodology.

Result/ Interpretations of Data

The data collected is discussed in the following tables along with their results and interpretations.

Growth rate

Table 1.1

S.No	1	2	3	4	5
Year	2007-08	2008-09	2009-10	2010-11	2011-12
Growth Rate (%)	9.3	6.7	8.6	9.3	6.2

Interpretation

From table (1.1) it is clear that the growth rate of Indian Economy has not been constant for last five years. In 2007-08 it was 9.3%, in 2008-09 it was decreased to 6.7%, in the yr. 2009-10 it was again increased to 8.6%, in 2010-11 it was increased sufficiently to 9.3% and in 2011-12 it was declined to 6.2%. Its graphical representation is given below in fig (1.1).

Figure 1.1

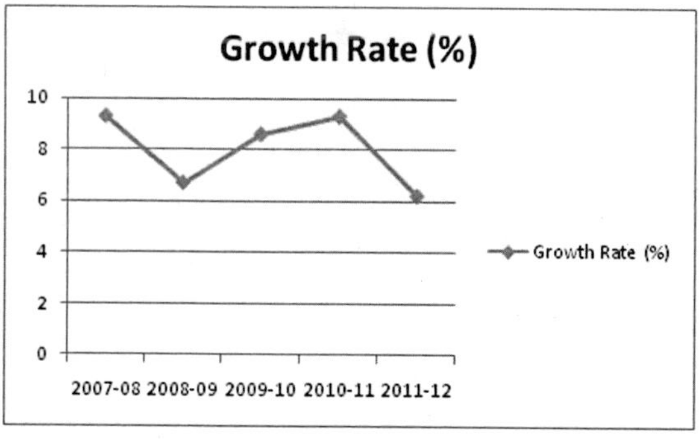

Per Capita Income

Table 1.2

S.No.	1	2	3	4	5
Year	**2007-08**	**2008-09**	**2009-10**	**2010-11**	**2011-12**
Per Capita Income (Rs)	35825	40775	46249	54151	61564

Interpretation

From table (1.2) it is clear that the per capita income of India have increased from Rs 35825 to Rs 61564, showing almost double from 2007-08, with every year increase in other years. Its graphical representation is given below in fig (1.2).

Figure.2

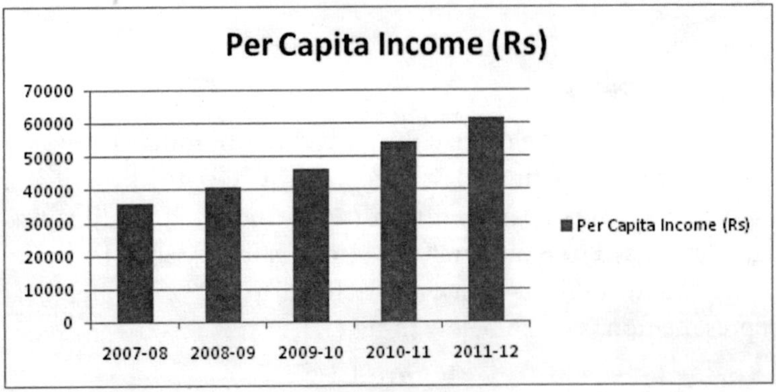

Production

Table (1.3)

S. No	1	2	3	4	5
Year	2007-08	2008-09	2009-10	2010-11	2011-12
Production (Million Tons)	230.8	234.5	218.1	244.5	259.3

Interpretation

From table (1.3) it is clear that the production in food grains in India has increased from 2007-08 to 2008-09 (230.8 million tons to 234.5 million tons) then it sharply decreases to 218.1 million tons in 2009-10 and again after 2009-10 to 2011-12 it goes on increasing from 218.1 million tons to 259.3 million tons. Its graphical representation is given below in fig (1.3).

Figure (1.3)

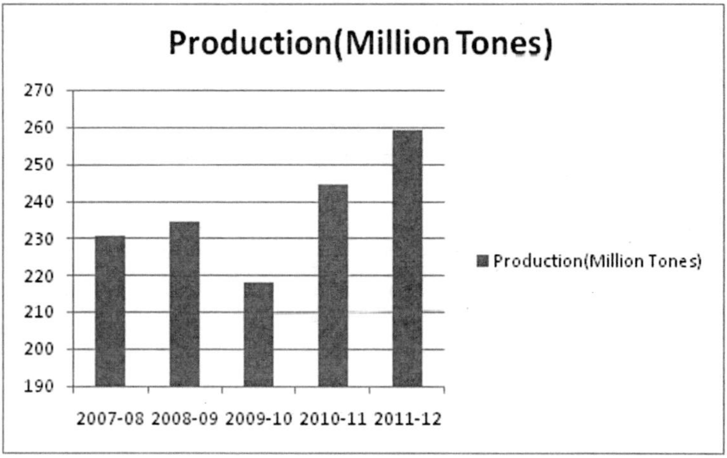

Inflation

Table (1.4)

S.No	1	2	3	4	5
Year	2007	2008	2009	2010	2011
Inflation (%)	6.4	8.3	10.9	11.7	8.9

Interpretation

From table (1.4) it is clear that the inflation have increased from 2007 to 2010 i.e. 6.4% to 11.7%. But after 2010 it declines to 8.9% in 2011. Its graphical representation is given below in fig (1.4).

Figure (1.4)

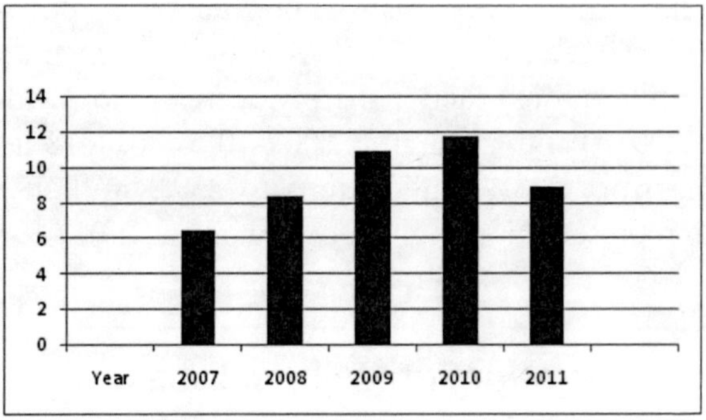

Export

Table (1.5)

S.No	1	2	3	4	5
Year	2007-08	2008-09	2009-10	2010-11	2011-12
Export (In Crores)	655864	840755	845534	1142922	1459286

Interpretation

From table (1.5) it is clear that the export of India have increased from 655864 crore to 1459286 crore, showing almost more than double from 2007-08, with every year increase in other years. Its graphical representation is given below in fig (1.5).

Figure 1.5

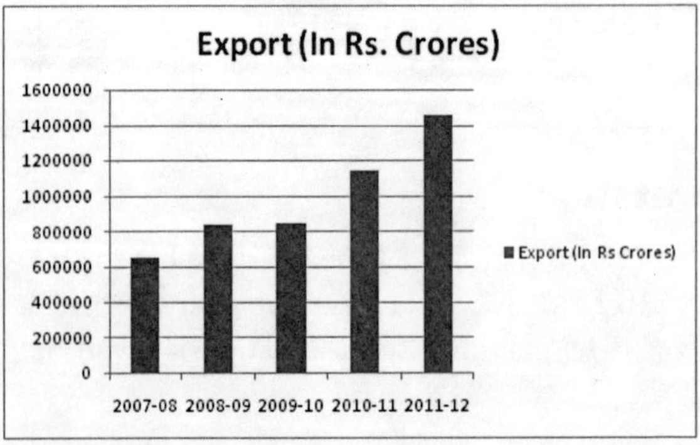

Import

Table (1.6)

S.No	1	2	3	4	5
Year	2007-08	2008-09	2009-10	2010-11	2011-12
Import (In Crores)	1012312	1374436	1363736	1683467	2344772

Interpretation

From table (1.3) it is clear that the import in India has increased from 2007-08 to 2008-09 (1012312 crore to 1374436 crore) then it sharply decreases to 1363736 crore in 2009-10 and again after 2009-10 to 2011-12 it goes on increasing (1363736 crore to 2344772 crore). Its graphical representation is given below in fig (1.6).

Figure (1.6)

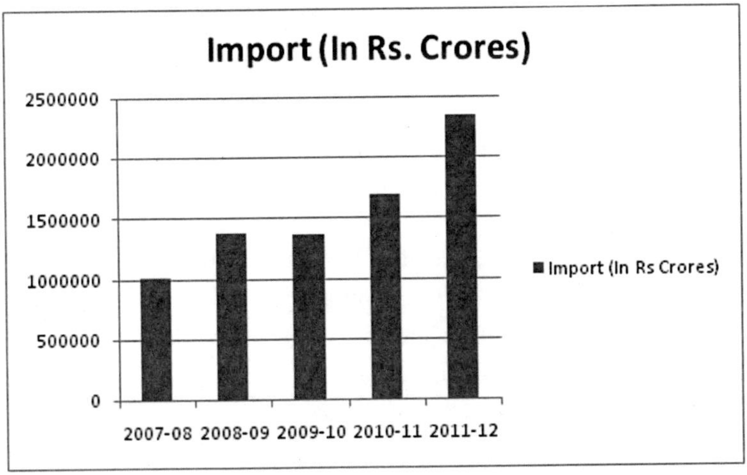

Findings of the Stud

It is observed that growth rate at current market price has been fluctuating from last five years.

It is clear that there is steady increase in per capita income.

There is an increase in the production in food grains in India from 2007-08 to 2010-11 except 2009-10.

It is observed that there is steady increase in the inflation from 2007 to 2010, but after 2010 it decrease's.

It is clear that there is increase in Export from 2007-11.

There is an increase in Import from 2007 to 2011 except 2009-10.

Conclusion

From the figures stated above it is clear that growth rate at current market price has been fluctuating from last five years, there is steady increase in per capita income and Export. There is an increase in the production in food grains and Import in India from 2007-08 to 2010-11 except 2009-10.

References/Websites

[1] Economic Survey 2012-13.

[2] Global Economics Paper No: 99- Dreaming with BRICs: The path to 2050.

[3] International Monetary Fund Retrieved 2013-04-16.

[4] The India Model, by Das, Gurcharan. 1936. Foreign Affairs, Vol. 85, No. 4 (Jul. – Aug. 2006), p.

[5] The Economist. 30 September 2010. Retrieved 2010-09-30.

[6] http://en.wikipedia.org/wiki/Economy_of_India

[7] http://indiabudget.nic.in/survey.asp

Table: 1.1, 1.2, 1.3, 1.4, 1.5 and 1.6.

Figures: 1.1, 1.2, 1.3, 1.4, 1.5 and 1.6.

Performance Evaluation of Public Sector Banks With Special Reference to Non-Performing Assets

Amit Kumar*
Research Scholar
Department of Commerce
Himachal Pradesh University, Shimla 171005

Abstract

In the present scenario, banking sector plays an important role in the development of the economy. The banking sector is facing the problem of increasing number of non- performing assets. The unprecedented rise in non-performing assets in public sector banks of India is major issue to concern in this sector. Non Performing Assets means a loan or an account of borrower, which has been classified as a sub-standard, doubtful or loss asset, in accordance with the directions or guidelines of asset classification issued by RBI. The study focuses on to examine the trend of nonperforming assets in major public sector banks. The study will also make a comparative analysis of NPAs in between these public sector banks and study the impact of NPAs on the performance of these public sector banks. The study will be based on the secondary data which will be collected through different relevant sources.

Keywords: NPAs, Banks

Introduction

The incidence of non-performing assets (NPAs) is affecting the performance of the credit institutions both financially and psychologically. Non-performing assets (NPAs) is not only non-performing but also makes the banker and the bank non-performing as it:

- Prevents or delays recycling of funds.
- denies income from the asset by way of interest
- Erodes profit by way of provisions.

NPAs is a disorder resulting in non-performance of a portion of loan portfolio leading to no recovery or less recovery / income to the lender. NPAs represent the quantified "Credit Risk". It also plays havoc on the mental make-up of the banker where in the banker tries to go slow on lending, fearing future NPAs, it may lead to delay and denial of credit resulting in low off- take of lendable funds.

NPAs are an inevitable burden on the banking industry. Hence, the success of a bank depends upon the methods of managing NPAs and keeping them within tolerance level. The concept of NPAs originated when Reserve Bank of India introduced 'prudential norms, on the recommendations of the Narashimam Committee in the year 1992-93.

As per the prudential norms laid down by RBI," An asset is considered as "non-performing" if interest on instalments of principal due remain unpaid for more than180 days (from March31,2004, it has been decided to adopt the ,90 days, overdue norm for identification of NPAs). Growth of non-performing assets on the balance sheet of banks erodes the solvency, profitability and financial health of banks. With a view to moving towards international best practices and to ensure greater transparency, 90 days overdue norm for identification of NPAs instead of 180 days has been adopted from the year ending March 31st 2004. Accordingly, a non-performing asset would be a loan or an advance where:

- interest and /or instalment of principal remain overdue for a period of more than 90 days, in respect of a term loan;
- the account remain ¸out of order, in respect of overdraft/ cash credit;
- the bill remain overdue for a period of more than 90 days in case of bill purchased and discounted; interest and or instalment of principal remains overdue for two harvest seasons but for a period not exceeding two half years in the case of an advance granted for agricultural purposes; and
- Any amount to be received remains overdue for a period of more than 90 days in respect of other accounts.(Any amount due to the bank under any credit facility is "Overdue" if it is not paid on the due date fixed by the bank).

Banks have been advised by the RBI that they should identify the non-performing assets and ensure that interest on such assets is not recognized as income and taken to the profit and loss account. Banks are to recognize their income on accrual basis in respect of income on performing assets and on cash basis in respect of income on non-performing assets. Any interest accrued and credited to income account must be cancelled by a reserve entry once the credit facility comes under the category of non-performing assets.

Gross and Net

Gross NPAs is an advance which is considered irrecoverable, for bank has made provisions, and which is still held in banks books of account.Net NPAs are obtained from gross NPAs after deduction of the following:

- Interest due but not received: i.e. balances in interest suspense account.
- Claims received from credit guarantors and kept in suspense accounts pending final settlement.
- Part payment received and kept in suspensions ;and
- Total provisions held.

- Similarly gross advances consists of bills purchased and discounted, cash credits, overdrafts and loans and term loans, whereas net advance is calculated by netting out bills discounted, DICGC claims etc., from gross advances. Gross NPA is a better indicator than net NPAs since the former does not incorporate the endogenous provisioning process; this is because banks make provisioning for NPAs according to their capacities.Net NPAs does not present a true picture of NPAs so they will have to be supplemented by gross NPAs figures.1

Review of Literature

Mahesh, Meenakshi, Rajeev (2010)2 argued that The NPAs is the root cause of the global financial crisis that we observed recently. The problem of NPAs has received considerable attention after the liberalisation of the financial sector in India. The study shows that such decline is mainly due to the awareness of the problem of bad loans at the bank level It remains true that NPAs in the priority sector is still higher than that of the non-priority sector. Kaur and Singh (2011)3 observed that the NPAs have always been a big worry for the banks in India. It is just not a problem for the banks; they are bad for the economy too. The money locked up in NPAs is not available for productive use and adverse effect on banks' profitability is there. The extent of NPAs is comparatively higher in public sectors banks. To improve the efficiency and profitability, the NPAs have to be scheduled. Jain, Sheikh, Nasreen (2012)4 examine the relationship between the banking industry and selected private banks in addition to this it also study the performance of loans, net profit and NPAs. Banks mainly make profit from the difference of interest received and loans paid. The paper shows movement of NPAs, Loans, and Net Profit of the private banking industry. Kumar and Singh (2012)5 analysed that the main reason of high percentage of NPAs is the target-oriented approach, which deteriorates the qualitative aspect of lending. NPAs put detrimental impact on the profitability, capital adequacy ratio and credibility of banks.

Chatterjee, Jeet and Das (2012)6 examined that the NPAs have a negative influence on the achievement of capital adequacy level, funds mobilization and deployment policy, banking system credibility, productivity and overall economy. Balasubramaniam and Gawde7 reviewed the trend of NPAs followed by a series of in-depth analyses on the high level of borrowings from banking sector indicating a build-up of sectored credit booms in general and also raising concerns about financial performance and operations of the borrowers. The third part dwells on the impact of restructuring of advances by banks on the basis of asset classification. Finally, certain issues and perspectives/challenges on the performance of banking sector and financial stability of the economy emerge conclusion.

Need of the Study

The Indian banking system has gone through significant reforms. The banking sector are witnessed the gradual increase in nonperforming assets that is a symbol of stagnant economy due to uncovered or nonperforming of lending of banks. So, this paper focuses to examine the impact of Net NPAs on Net profits of the banks. An attempt has also been made to study the trend of Nonperforming assets in public sector banks. In the present study, top five public sector commercial banks have been taken on the basic of their market capitalization. The study is based on the secondary data. The data is collected from annual reports of the banks. The study is based on the five years financial data of the banks viz. 2008-09 to 2012-13. The banks taken in the study are State Bank of India, Bank of Baroda, Punjab National Bank, Bank of India and Canara Bank. The main focus of the study is to examine the impact of Nonperforming assets on Net profitability of the bank.

Objective

- To examine the impact of Nonperforming assets on Net profitability of the bank

- To study the trend of Nonperforming assets in public sector banks.

Methodology

The present study is aims to analyze the NPAs and Net profit of five public Banks. For the purpose of the study data has been collected from secondary sources. The main source of information has been through annual reports published by commercial banks in each financial year.

Analysis and Discussion

The table 1 shows the financial performance of top five public sector banks in India Viz. State Bank of India, Bank of Baroda, Punjab National Bank, Bank of India and Canara Bank in terms of Net Profit after tax and Non Performing assets. The trend is also shown through bar diagram.

State Bank of India

The State Bank of India is one of the largest public sector bank in India its profit shows the increasing trend during the study period except in 2011. It is 9121.23 crore in 2009, 9166.05 crore in 2010, 11707 crore in 2012 and 14105 crore in 2013. The non performing asset of the SBI also shows rapid increase in the year 2011, 2012 and 2013. It is clear from the table that the profit has been increased in all the years except 2011 but on the other side the non performing assets shows a repaid increase in these years. It is an alarming sign to state bank of India because non-performing assets in the bank per year increasing more than the net profit of bank.

Bank of Baroda

The Bank of Baroda is second largest public sector bank in India in the term of market capitalisation. The net profit of the Bank of Baroda is rise with good rate till year 2012 but it decrease in the year 2013. The profits were 2227.20 crore in 2009, 3058.33 crore in 2010, 4241.68 crore in 2011, 5006.96 crore in 2012 and decrease up to 4480.72 crore in the year 2013. The non performing assets of the bank rise steadily till the year 2011, and in the year 2012 and 2013 they has been risen at rapidly. They were 451.15 crore in 2009, 602.32 crore in 2010, 790.88 crore in 2011, 1543.64 crore in 2012 and 4192.02 crore in 2013. It depicts that Instantaneous jump in the non performing assets is not a good sign for the growth of bank of Baroda.

Punjab National Bank

The Punjab National Bank is the one of the leading public sector bank in India. The table depicts that the net profit was 3090.88 crore in 2009, 3905.35 crore in 2010, 4433.49 crore in 2011, 4884.20 crore in2012, 4747.67 crore in 2013. It clarify that the net profit of PNB was rise in 2010 but after that it was increased with decreasing rate till 2012 and after it was decreased in the year2013. The non performing assets of the bank was 263.86 crore in the year 2009, 981.69 crore in the year2010, 2038.63 crore in the year 2011, 4454.23 crore in the year 2012, 7236.50 crore in the year2013. The net profit of the bank has not been risen in proportion to net NPAs which shows poor financial performance of the bank.

Table 1 Nonperforming Assets and Net Profit of Five Public Sector Banks

2013		
Public Sector Bank	NET NPA	NET PROFIT
State Bank of India	21956.48	14105
Bank of Baroda	4192.02	4480.72
Punjab National Bank	7236.50	4747.67
Bank of India	5947	2749.34
Canara Bank	5278.07	2872 .10
Average	8922.014	5790.966

2012		
Public Sector Bank	NET NPA	NET PROFIT
State Bank of India	15818.85	11707
Bank of Baroda	1543.64	5006.96
Punjab National Bank	4454.23	4884.20
Bank of India	3656	2677.51
Canara Bank	3386.31	3282.71
Average	5771.80	5511.676
2011		
Public Sector Bank	NET NPA	NET PROFIT
State Bank of India	12346.90	8265
Bank of Baroda	790.88	4241.68
Punjab National Bank	2038.63	4433.49
Bank of India	1945	2488.70
Canara Bank	2329.91	4025.88
Average	3890.264	4690.95
2010		
Public Sector Bank	NET NPA	NET PROFIT
State Bank of India	10870.17	9166.05
Bank of Baroda	602.32	3058.33
Punjab National Bank	981.69	3905.35
Bank of India	2207.45	1741.07
Canara Bank	1799.70	3021.43
Average	3292.266	4178.446
2009		
Public Sector Bank	NET NPA	NET PROFIT
State Bank of India	9677.42	9121.23
Bank of Baroda	451.15	2227.20
Punjab National Bank	263.86	3090.88
Bank of India	628.21	3007.35
Canara Bank	1507.25	2072.42

Average	2505.578	3903.816
Average		
Public Sector Bank	NPA	NET PROFIT
State Bank of India	14133.96	10472.86
Bank of Baroda	1516.00	3802.98
Punjab National Bank	2994.98	4212.32
Bank of India	2876.73	2532.79
Canara Bank	2860.25	3054.91
Average	4960.67	4815.17

Note:- The Figures shown in the table are in crore), Net profit in the table is after tax.

Source: - Data taken from annual report Published by the Bank

Bank of India

The Bank of India is fourth number bank in term of market capitalisation. The net profit of Bank of India was 3007.35 crore in the year 2009, 1741.07 crore in the year 2010, 2488.70 crore in the year 2011, 2677.51 crore in the year 2012, 2749.34 crore in the year 2013. The net profit of the bank has been decline in the year 2010 after that it has been increased steadily in the year 2011, 2012 and 2013. The non performing assets of the BOI was quickly rise in the year 2010 up to 2207.45 crore after that it decreased to 1945 crore after that it show instant rising trend in the year2012 (3656crore) and in the year 2013 (5947 crore). The net profit and NPA, both of BOI are fluctuated during study period but net NPA risen more the net profit. It is not good sign for healthy growth of bank.

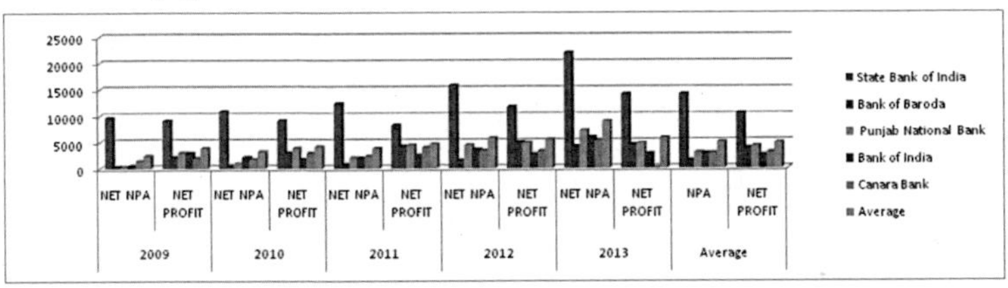

Note: - Value are shown in crore

Canara Bank

The table describe that the net profit of Canara bank, fifth largest public sector bank in the term of market capitalisation in India, have been in the year 2009 (3903.816 crore) and after that it risen gradually during the period 2010 (4178.446 crore), in the year 2011 (4690.95 crore), in the year 2012 it has been increased quickly up to 5511.676 crore and in the year 2013 it rise slowly and reached up to 5790.966 crore. The non performing assets of Canara bank risen bit by bit till in the 2011, it was 2505.578 crore in the year 2009, 3292.266 crore in the year 2010, 3890.264 crore in the year 2011, and shows significant rise in the year 2012 (5771.80 crore) and in the year 2013 (8922.014 crore). The non performing assets of the bank has risen significantly in recent years but growth rate in the profit slowdown in these years this is a sign of poor financial management.

2. Common Size Statement of Public Sector Banks

The table 2 illustrate that the common size statement of top five public sector banks. The comparative trend of NPAs also shown through Line diagram. The common size statement demonstrate that State Bank of India constitute major part of the profit and explain decline trend in the year of (43.87 percent) in the year 2010 as comparison to (46.73 percent) in the year 2009 and in the year 2011 (35.24 percent) in comparison to previous year. It has been increased (42.48percent) in the year 2012 and shows largest rise in the year 2013 (48.71 percent) in recent three year. SBI also comprise major part of NPA among the available NPAs of five public sector banks.

Table 2 Common Size Statement of Public Sector Banks

2013		
Public Sector Bank	NET NPA	NET PROFIT
State Bank of India	49.22	48.71

Bank of Baroda	9.40	15.47
Punjab National Bank	16.22	16.40
Bank of India	13.33	9.50
Canara Bank	11.83	9.92
Total	100	100
2012		
Public Sector Bank	NET NPA	NET PROFIT
State Bank of India	54.81	42.48
Bank of Baroda	5.35	18.17
Punjab National Bank	15.43	17.72
Bank of India	12.67	9.72
Canara Bank	11.73	11.91
Total	100	100
2011		
Public Sector Bank	NET NPA	NET PROFIT
State Bank of India	63.48	35.24
Bank of Baroda	4.07	18.08
Punjab National Bank	10.48	18.90
Bank of India	10.00	10.61
Canara Bank	11.98	17.16
Total	100	100
2010		
Public Sector Bank	NET NPA	NET PROFIT
State Bank of India	66.03	43.87
Bank of Baroda	3.66	14.64
Punjab National Bank	5.96	18.69
Bank of India	13.41	8.33
Canara Bank	10.20	14.46
Total	100	100

2009		
Public Sector Bank	NET NPA	NET PROFIT
State Bank of India	9677.42	9121.23
Bank of Baroda	451.15	2227.20
Punjab National Bank	263.86	3090.88
Bank of India	628.21	3007.35
Canara Bank	1507.25	2072.42
Total	2505.578	3903.816

Note:- Figures in the table are in percentage

The non performing assets of SBI shows gradually decline trend in the period in between 2009 to 2010 in proportion to total NPA of five public sector banks. It has been 77.25 percent in the year 2009, 66.03 percent in the year 2010, percent in the year 2011, and 54.81 percent in the year 2012, 49.22 percent in the year 2013. The net profit of Bank of Baroda shows rising trend in the year 2010 (14.64 percent) it was 11.41 percent in the year 2009, in the year 2011 (18.08 percent) and in the year 2012 (18.17 percent) and decreased in the year 2013 (15.47 percent). The nonperforming assets of the Bank of Baroda have been risen slowly in the initial period and speed up in the last two year in fraction to total NPA.

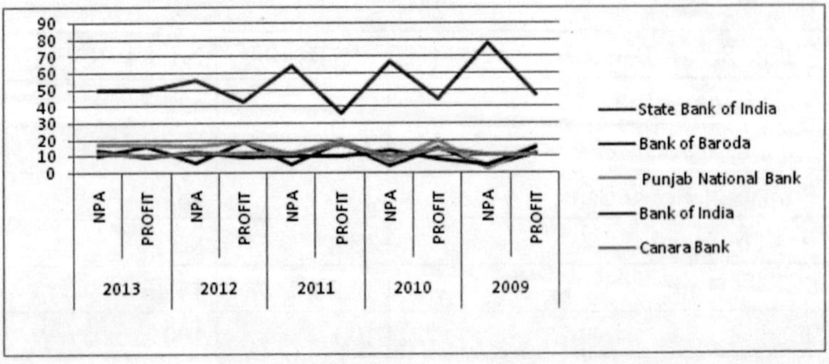

The Punjab national bank's net profit shows rising trend in the first three years and after that it has been decline in the year 2012

and 2013. The non performing assets of Punjab National Bank have been showing regular rising trend in proportion to total NPA of five public sector banks. The net profit of Bank of India showing fluctuating trend during the study period it has been decreased in the year 2010 and rise again in 2011 and after that it has been declining gradually. The nonperforming assets of the Bank of India shows rising trend in the year 2010 and after that it have been declined step by step. The table shows rising trend in net profit of Canara Bank in the year 2010, 2011, and it has been declined in the year 2012 and 2013. The non performing assets of Canara bank have been decline in the year 2010 after that it shows stagnant trend in the proportion to total NPA of top five public sector bank.

Table 3 Sector –Wise NPAs (in percentage to Total advances per Bank) of five Public Sector Banks for the period 2009 to 2013

Sectors/Bank	State Bank of India				
	2013	2012	2011	2010	2009
Agriculture & allied activities	9.50	8.92	6.74	2.60	NA
Industry (Micro & Small, Medium and Large)	4.37	4.12	2.80	3.89	NA
Services	4.43	2.94	2.93	3.91	NA
Personal Loans	1.98	2.92	2.54	2.90	NA

Sectors/Bank	Bank of Baroda				
	2013	2012	2011	2010	2009
Agriculture & allied activities	4.91	3.99	3.47	3.33	1.55
Industry (Micro & Small, Medium and Large)	3.31	1.12	1.76	1.06	.92
Services	5.27	2.72	1.22	.82	1.18
Personal Loans	6.87	3.66	1.72	3.68	4.85

Sectors/Bank	Punjab National Bank				
	2013	2012	2011	2010	2009
Agriculture & allied activities	6.33	5.03	3.62	3.65	NA
Industry (Micro & Small, Medium and Large)	5.47	2.86	1.70	.92	NA
Services	2.80	3.46	1.44	1.93	NA
Personal Loans	3.31	2.54	1.92	2.18	NA

Sectors/Bank	Bank of India				
	2013	2012	2011	2010	2009
Agriculture & allied activities	2.02	2.17	2.94	2.36	NA
Industry (Micro & Small, Medium and Large)	4.82	1.90	2.56	3.09	NA
Services	2.96	3.57	2.29	4.74	NA
Personal Loans	1.30	2.56	4.30	4.16	NA

Sectors/Bank	Canara Bank				
	2013	2012	2011	2010	2009
Agriculture & allied activities	2.17	2.13	2.27	1.84	NA
Industry (Micro & Small, Medium and Large)	1.96	1.37	1.07	0.77	NA
Services	6.93	1.83	Nil	0.00	NA
Personal Loans	1.88	4.92	5.12	5.95	NA

Note:- Figures in the table are in percentage

The table 3 shows that sector-wise lending of five public sector banks for the period 2009 to 2013.

State Bank of India

The maximum nonperforming assets of State bank of India are in agriculture and allied activity and shows quick rise in the period 2011 and it has been grow at lesser rate in the period 2012 and

2013. Industrial sector also shows continues rise at lesser rate of NPA. The service sector shows decline in NPA in the period 2011 and is also stagnant for the period 2012 but risen quickly in the year 2013. The NPAs in personal loan have been stagnant in the period 2010, 2011, 2012 and it decline in the year 2013.

Bank of Baroda

The personal loan of bank of Baroda shows maximum nonperforming assets in the year 2009, 2010, and 2013 and second number sector for the NPAs in the period 2012. Agriculture & allied activities and Industrial sector depict gradual increase in NPA during the period. The NPA in service sector has been decreased in the period 2010 after that it increased with two fold growth rate.

Punjab National Bank

Agriculture & allied activities and Industrial sector of Punjab national Bank show regular increase in the non performing assets during the study period. Services sector's NPAs show decline in the year 2011 but rise again in the year 2012 and thereafter decreased in the year 2013. The NPAs in the personal loan decrease in the 2011 and it has been risen in the year 2012 and 2013.

Bank of India

Agriculture & allied activities sector's nonperforming assets show steady decline after the year 2011. Nonperforming assets in the industrial sector declined in the year 2011, 2012 and increased in the year 2013. Nonperforming assets in the service and personal loan sectors show fluctuation in the study period.

Canara Bank

The non performing assets in the Agriculture & allied activities shows increase in the year 2011 and stagnant in the subsequent year. Industrial sector's NPAs in gradual increase over the study period. The non performing assets in Service sector increased instantly in the year 2011. The NPAs in Personal Loans shows declining trend during the period.

Conclusion

It is concluded that the Nonperforming assets of the major public sector are increasing step by step. The Net Profit of the banks showing fluctuating trend during last five year. The unbalanced growth of Net profit in comparison to NPAs demonstrate that the inefficient financial police of the banks.SBI as top bank in the term of capitalisation also got top place in the term of NPAs among the top five public sector bank. The major NPAs of the Public Sector banks are in the agriculture sector which one of the worst performing sector of the economy. On the other hand industrial sector also shows increasing trend in NPAs. The NPAs in the service sector also depicts increasing trend during the period in spite of major contributor in the GDP of the country. It indicates that the bank does not have appropriate procedure for projects appraisal.

Suggestions

To reduce the growing problems of NPAs in the banks it is suggested that:-

1. The lending policy of the banks must be clear and well documented to customer.
2. Banks should seriously examine the causes of defaulter and make changing accordingly to their polices.
3. During lending period the bank must built appropriate procedure to analyse the creditworthiness of the Borrowers and feasibility of the projects.
4. Banks should approach for apposite collateral security for the loan. So that In case defaulter the collateral security could be used.
5. The review of the projects, which have to be financed, at regular interval should be exercised by the bank and payment must be made in instalments after the periodical review of the projects, if

the progress is satisfactorily.

6. The recovery system of the bank should be flexible and it must be according to nature of the project.
7. The banks should develop healthy recovery competition among the recovery staff members to get rid of loophole of policies. The member with highest amount of recovery should be rewarded.
8. The bank must periodically study the trend of nonperforming accounts.
9. The bank should limit lending to the sector which results high NPAs and least profit.

References

1) www.cpmr.org.in
2) Mahesh H P, Meenakshi, Rajeev (2010) "Banking Sector Reforms and NPA: A study of Indian Commercial Banks" Working paper 252, The Institute for Social and Economic Change.
3) Kaur Kamalpreet and Singh Balraj (2011), "Non-Performing Assets of Public And Private Sector Banks (A Comparative Study)", South Asian Journal of Marketing & Management Research Volume 1, Issue 3 (December, 2011)
4) Jain. Dhiraj, Sheikh .Nasreen (2012) "A Comparative Study of Loan Performance, NPAs And Net Profit In Selected Indian Private Banks", International Journal of Marketing, Financial Services & Management Research Vol.1 Issue 9, September 2012, ISSN 2277 3622
5) Kumar Mohan, Singh Govind (2012), "Mounting NPAs In Indian Commercial Banks" , International Journal of Transformations in Business Management, Vol. No. 1, Issue No. 6,2012
6) Chatterjee Chandan, Mukherjee Jeet and Das Ratan (2012) "Management of Non Performing Assets - A Current Scenario", IRJC International Journal of Social Science & Interdisciplinary Research Vol.1 Issue 11, November 2012
7) Balasubramaniam C.S. and Gawde Babasaheb "Non Performing Assets and Profitability of Commercial Banks In India: Assessment and Emerging Issues" www.abhinavjournal.com

Globalization and Banking Reforms in India

Dr. Ajay Kumar Chaudhary

Associate Professor, Government College Nagrota Bagwan, Distt. Kangra (H.P.)

E-mail. ajydoctor@hotmail.com

Abstrct

The term globalization we mean opening up of the economy for world market by attaining international competitiveness. The globalization of the economy simply indicates interaction of the country relating to production, trading and financial transactions with the developed industrialised countries of the world. The term globalization has four parameters i.e. permitting free flow of goods by removing or reducing trade barriers between the countries, creating environment for flow of capital between the countries, allowing free flow of technology transfer and creating environment for free movement of labour between the countries of the world. There are three distinct spells of development of banking industry in post independent India, the pre-nationalization era from 1947 to 1969, the post-nationalization cum preliberalization era from 1969 to 1991 and the neo-liberalization era from 1991 onwards. The first phase was mostly city-centric private banking marked by frequent failures and liquidation of banks and consequent pauperization of numerous poor and middle class depositors and loss of jobs for the employees. The post-nationalization era saw a sea change in the banking scenario: financial stability of Public Sector Banks controlling more than 80% of banking business of the country,

PSBs commanding trust and confidence of the banking-public, expansion of branch net-work of banks – particularly in hitherto unbanked rural and semi-urban centres, opening up the banking services accessible to the rural poor, expansion of credit to agriculture, small scale industries and small entrepreneurs, artisans – even to the marginal farmers, small shop owners, vegetable vendors etc. With the impact of Globalization onset of World Bank-IMF dictated reforms, euphemistically called liberalization, successive Governments at the centre have consistently been trying to undo all the good work of the public sector banks as also to dismantle and privatize the public sector banks altogether.

Introduction

There are three distinct spells of development of banking industry in post independent India, the pre-nationalization era from 1947 to 1969, the post-nationalization cum pre-liberalization era from 1969 to 1991 and the neo-liberalization era from 1991 onwards. The first phase was mostly city-centric private Banking marked by frequent failures and liquidation of Banks and consequent pauperization of numerous poor and middle class depositors and loss of jobs for the employees. The post-nationalization era saw a sea change in the Banking scenario financial stability of Public Sector Banks (PSBs) controlling more than 84% of Banking business of the country, PSBs commanding trust and confidence of the Banking-public, expansion of Branch net-work of Banks –particularly in hitherto unbanked rural and semi-urban centres, opening up the banking services accessible to the rural poor, expansion of credit to agriculture, small scale industries and small entrepreneurs, artisans – even to the marginal farmers, small shop owners, vegetable vendors etc. Such expansion of Branch network, coupled with such mass-banking, created considerable job opportunities on the one hand, and, on the other, it helped a green revolution on the agricultural sector, obviating dependence of import of food grains, as also a spurt in the development of Small and Medium Scale Industries. It also rescued a vast section of the rural poor from the exploitation by village-money-lenders. By tapping the hitherto untapped huge rural savings, the PSBs could help the growth of large scale and capital intensive industries too. During this post nationalization era, Regional Rural Banks (RRBs) were established in 1975 onwards under the auspices of PSBs to cater to the credit needs of rural-India. Till 1990, priority sector lending constituted over 70% of the advance portfolio of RRBs giving further fillip to the rural economy. With the onset of World Bank-IMF dictated reforms, euphemistically called liberalization, successive Governments at the centre have consistently been trying to undo all the good work of the PSBs as also to dismantle and privatize the PSBs altogether. On 14th August 1991, the Government of India (GOI) appointed a Committee headed by Mr. M. Narashimham (called "Narashimham Committee – I") to suggest the modus operandi for reforms of the Banking Sector. On 16th November 1991, the said Committee submitted its Report suggesting downsizing of PSBs through closure of Branches, merger of PSBs, reduction of priority sector lending from the then prevailing 40% to 10% of total advance portfolio, abolition of Banking Service Recruitment Board, granting of more autonomy to PSBs in respect of both financial and administrative matters, to reduce the supervisory and regulatory control of Reserve Bank of India (RBI), the Central Bank of the country, and, to top it all, dilution of Government Holding in PSBs through suitable amendment of relevant legislations. Thereafter, a number of committees, such as Narashimham Committee – II, Khan Committee, Verma Committee, S.C.Gupta Committee, Raghuram Rajan Committee, Anwarul Hoda Committee, to name a few, have been appointed to assess the progress in implementation of the Recommendations of the "Narashimham Committee – I" as also to suggest measures for carrying forward the reforms of the Banking Sector further as per dictates of the World Bank-IMF.

Objectives of The Paper

The main objectives of the present paper are:

- To analyze the trends of globalization in India.
- To examine the impact of globalization in India.
- To study the banking system in India.
- To analyze the role of globalization and its impact on banking system.
- To highlight challenges and threats.

Research Methodology

Data Collection:

The data for the said study is collected from the secondary sources as per past studies, Government circulars, notifications, publications of national and international organizations. The collected data may be tabulated as per requirements.

Globalization

The term globalization is imprecise and contested. For those emphasising economic globalization, the main part of the package is increasing integration of the global economy through product and factor markets by way of trade, direct investment and financial flows, greatly aided by deregulation of markets and the liberalisation of trade and capital movements. Many in the Asia-Pacific region would like to limit globalization's effects to economics, as the quote from China's President implies, but while associated impacts can be limited they cannot be totally controlled. While economic aspects remain central, globalization embraces more, if less precise, transformations through the associated spread of information, perceptions and ideas. These latter influences, in particular, have themselves provided the organisational flexibility that leads to various characteristics of economic globalization. Discussions of the implications of globalization are equally imprecise, in part because it combines different processes. That these different processes are incomplete is illustrated by the argument that we should speak of a 'globalizing process' rather than 'globalization'. Although the international market has become global with the end of the Cold War, it is not fully integrated. In a fully integrated global market, the 'law of one price' would apply, meaning that any commodity has the same price throughout the world. This seems to hold for basic commodities such as wheat but the evidence is less clear for non-standard products such as motor vehicles that, even within the European Union, have different wholesale and retail mark-ups. Moreover, the market for investment funds seems similarly substantially local. Capital still does not flow completely to the most profitable investment sites; most savings are still invested in the saving country. Nevertheless, globalizing changes are occurring and, together with other processes of modernisation, such as the spread of capitalistic productive processes, have been facilitated by technological changes in information, communications and transport technologies. The Internet, global communication networks, such as CNN, and global money, from credit cards to derivatives, have been major influences. In addition, global and regional institutions, such as the United Nations and the Asia Pacific Economic Cooperation (APEC) forum, have helped by bringing much of the international community together, sharing information, understandings and more especially, ideas. Clearly, as already noted, there is much more to globalization than economic changes. The international connections include as well as economics and technologies, social, political and cultural links that, as with the economic and technology links, increasingly tend to override territorial, legal and political barriers and change the nature of political and social governance.

Worldwide Banking System

A bank is a financial institution and a financial intermediary that accepts deposits and channels those deposits into lending activities, either directly by loaning or indirectly through capital markets. A bank links together customers that have capital deficits and customers with capital surpluses. Due to their influential status within the financial system and upon national economies, banks are highly regulated in most countries. Most nations have institutionalised a system known as fractional reserve banking, in which banks hold only a small reserve of the funds deposited and lend out the rest for profit. They are generally subject to minimum capital requirements based on an international set of capital standards, known as the Basel Accords. Banking in its modern sense evolved in the 14th century in the rich cities of Renaissance Italy but in many ways was a continuation of ideas and concepts of credit and lending that had its roots in the ancient world. In the history of banking, a number of banking dynasties have played a central role over many centuries. Merchants started to store their gold with the goldsmiths of London, who possessed private vaults, and charged a fee for that service. In exchange for each deposit of precious metal, the goldsmiths issued receipts certifying the quantity and purity of the metal they held as a bailee; these receipts could not be assigned, only the original depositor could collect the stored goods. The sealing of the Bank of England Charter (1694). Gradually the goldsmiths began to lend the money out on behalf of the depositor, which led to the development of modern banking practices; promissory notes (which evolved into banknotes) were issued for money deposited as a loan to the goldsmith. The goldsmith paid interest on these deposits. Since the promissory notes were payable on demand, and the advances (loans) to the goldsmith's customers were repayable over a longer time period, this was an early form of fractional reserve banking. The promissory notes developed into an assignable instrument which could circulate as a safe and convenient form of money backed by the goldsmith's promise to pay, allowing goldsmiths to advance loans with little risk of default. Thus, the goldsmiths of London became the forerunners of banking by creating new money based on credit. The Bank of England was the first to begin the permanent issue of banknotes, in 1695. The Royal Bank of Scotland established the first overdraft facility in 1728. By the beginning of the 19th century a bankers' clearing house was established in London to allow multiple banks to clear transactions.

Banking Standard Activities

Banks act as payment agents by conducting checking or current accounts for customers, paying cheques drawn by customers on the bank, and collecting cheques deposited to customers' current accounts. Banks also enable customer payments via other payment methods such as Automated Clearing House (ACH), Wire transfers or telegraphic transfer, EFTPOS, and automated teller machine (ATM). Banks borrow money by accepting funds deposited on current accounts, by accepting term deposits, and by issuing debt securities such as banknotes and bonds. Banks lend money by making advances to customers on current accounts, by making instalment loans, and by investing in marketable debt securities and other forms of money lending. Banks provide different payment services, and a bank account is considered indispensable by most businesses and individuals. Non-banks that provide payment services such as remittance companies are normally not considered as an adequate substitute for a bank account. Banks can create new money when they make a loan. New loans throughout the banking system generate new deposits elsewhere in the system. The money supply is usually increased by the act of lending, and reduced when loans are repaid faster than new ones are generated. In the United Kingdom between 1997 and 2007, there was a big increase in the money supply, largely caused by much more bank lending, which served to push up property prices and increase private debt. Excessive or risky lending can cause borrowers to default, the banks then become more cautious, so there is less lending and therefore less money so that the economy can go from boom to bust as happened in the UK and many other Western economies after 2007.

Channels

Banks offer many different channels to access their banking and other services such as;

- Automated Teller Machines
- A branch is a retail location
- Call centre
- Mail: most banks accept cheque deposits via mail and use mail to communicate to their customers, e.g. by sending out statements
- Mobile banking is a method of using one's mobile phone to conduct banking transactions
- Online banking is a term used for performing multiple transactions, payments etc. over the Internet
- Relationship Managers, mostly for private banking or business banking, often visiting customers at their homes or businesses
- Telephone banking is a service which allows its customers to conduct transactions over the telephone with automated attendant or when requested with telephone operator
- Video banking is a term used for performing banking transactions or professional banking consultations via a remote video and audio connection. Video banking can be performed via purpose built banking transaction machines (similar to an Automated teller machine), or via a video conference enabled bank branch clarification
- DSA is a Direct Selling Agent, who works for the bank based on a contract. Its main job is to increase the customer base for the bank.

Globalization in the Banking Industry

In modern time there have been huge reductions to the barriers of global competition in the banking industry. Increases in telecommunications and other financial technologies have allowed banks to extend their reach all over the world, since they no longer have to be near customers to manage both their finances and their risk. The growth in cross-border activities has also increased the demand for banks that can provide various services across borders to different nationalities. However, despite these reductions in barriers and growth in cross-border activities, the banking industry is nowhere near as globalized as some other industries. One reason the banking industry has not been fully globalized is that it is more convenient to have local banks provide loans to small business and individuals. On the other hand for large corporations, it is not as important in what nation the bank is in, since the corporation's financial information is available around the globe. The history of banking begins with the first prototype banks of merchants of the ancient world, which made grain loans to farmers and traders who carried goods between cities. Later, in ancient Greece and during the Roman Empire, lenders based in temples made loans and added two important innovations: they accepted deposits and changed money. Archaeology from this period in ancient China and India also shows evidence of money lending activity. Banking, in the modern sense of the word, can be traced to medieval and early Renaissance Italy, to the rich cities in the north such as Florence, Venice and Genoa. The development of banking spread from northern Italy throughout the Holy Roman Empire, and in the 16th century the position of the Medicis was eventually taken over by the Fuggers and the Welsers, followed by a number of important innovations that took place in Amsterdam during the Dutch Republic in the 17th century, and in London in the 18th century. During the 20th century, developments in telecommunications and computing caused major changes to banks' operations and let banks dramatically increase in size and geographic spread. The financial crisis of 2007–2008 caused many bank failures, including some of the world's largest banks, and provoked much debate about bank regulation.

Banking System in India

Banking in India in the modern sense originated in the last decades of the 18th century. The first banks were Bank of

Hindustan (1770-1829) and The General Bank of India, established 1786 and since defunct. The largest bank, and the oldest still in existence, is the State Bank of India, which originated in the Bank of Calcutta in June 1806, which almost immediately became the Bank of Bengal. This was one of the three presidency banks, the other two being the Bank of Bombay and the Bank of Madras, all three of which were established under charters from the British East India Company. The three banks merged in 1921 to form the Imperial Bank of India, which, upon India's independence, became the State Bank of India in 1955. For many years the presidency banks acted as quasi-central banks, as did their successors, until the Reserve Bank of India was established in 1935. In 1969 the Indian government nationalised all the major banks that it did not already own and these have remained under government ownership. They are run under a structure known as 'profit-making public sector undertaking' (PSU) and are allowed to compete and operate as commercial banks. The Indian banking sector is made up of four types of banks, as well as the PSUs and the state banks; they have been joined since the 1990s by new private commercial banks and a number of foreign banks. Banking in India was generally fairly mature in terms of supply, product range and reach-even though reach in rural India and to the poor still remains a challenge. The government has developed initiatives to address this through the State bank of India expanding its branch network and through the National Bank for Agriculture and Rural Development with things like microfinance.

Colonial Era

During the period of British rule merchants established the Union Bank of Calcutta in 1829, first as a private joint stock association, then partnership. Its proprietors were the owners of the earlier Commercial Bank and the Calcutta Bank, who by mutual consent created Union Bank to replace these two banks. In 1840 it established an agency at Singapore, and closed the one at Mirzapore that it had opened in the previous year. Also in 1840 the Bank revealed that it had been the subject of a fraud by the bank's accountant. Union Bank was incorporated in 1845 but failed in 1848, having been insolvent for some time and having used new money from depositors to pay its dividends. The Allahabad Bank, established in 1865 and still functioning today, is the oldest Joint Stock bank in India. Calcutta was the most active trading port in India, mainly due to the trade of the British Empire, and so became a banking centre. The period between 1906 and 1911, saw the establishment of banks inspired by the Swadeshi movement. A number of banks established then have survived to the present such as Bank of India, Corporation Bank, Indian Bank, Bank of Baroda, Canara Bank and Central Bank of India.

Post-Independence

The partition of India in 1947 adversely impacted the economies of Punjab and West Bengal, paralysing banking activities for months. India's independence marked the end of a regime of the Laissez-faire for the Indian banking. The Government of India initiated measures to play an active role in the economic life of the nation, and the Industrial Policy Resolution adopted by the government in 1948 envisaged a mixed economy. This resulted into greater involvement of the state in different segments of the economy including banking and finance. The major steps to regulate banking included; The Reserve Bank of India, India's central banking authority, was established in April 1935, but was nationalised on 1 January 1949 under the terms of the Reserve Bank of India (Transfer to Public Ownership) Act, 1948. In 1949, the Banking Regulation Act was enacted which empowered the Reserve Bank of India (RBI) "to regulate, control, and inspect the banks in India".

Nationalization in the 1960s

Despite the provisions, control and regulations of the Reserve Bank of India, banks in India except the State Bank of India or

SBI, continued to be owned and operated by private persons. By the 1960s, the Indian banking industry had become an important tool to facilitate the development of the Indian economy. At the same time, it had emerged as a large employer, and a debate had ensued about the nationalization of the banking industry. Indira Gandhi, the then Prime Minister of India, expressed the intention of the Government of India in the annual conference of the All India Congress Meeting in a paper entitled "Stray thoughts on Bank Nationalization." The meeting received the paper with enthusiasm. Thereafter, her move was swift and sudden. The Government of India issued an ordinance ('Banking Companies (Acquisition and Transfer of Undertakings) Ordinance, 1969') and nationalised the 14 largest commercial banks with effect from the midnight of 19 July 1969. These banks contained 85 percent of bank deposits in the country. A second dose of nationalisation of 6 more commercial banks followed in 1980. The stated reason for the nationalisation was to give the government more control of credit delivery. With the second dose of nationalisation, the Government of India controlled around 91% of the banking business of India. Later on, in the year 1993, the government merged New Bank of India with Punjab National Bank. It was the only merger between nationalised banks and resulted in the reduction of the number of nationalised banks from 20 to 19. After this, until the 1990s, the nationalised banks grew at a pace of around 4% closer to the average growth rate of the Indian economy.

Liberalization in the 1990s

In the early 1990s, the then government embarked on a policy of liberalization, licensing a small number of private banks. These came to be known as New Generation tech-savvy banks, and included Global Trust Bank (the first of such new generation banks to be set up), which later amalgamated with Oriental Bank of Commerce, UTI Bank (since renamed Axis Bank), ICICI Bank and HDFC Bank. This move, along with the rapid growth in the economy of India, revitalised the banking sector in India, which has seen rapid growth with strong contribution from all the three sectors of banks, namely, government banks, private banks and foreign banks. The next stage for the Indian banking has been set up with the proposed relaxation in the norms for Foreign Direct Investment, where all Foreign Investors in banks may be given voting rights which could exceed the present cap of 10%, at present it has gone up to 74% with some restrictions.

Current Period

By 2010, banking in India was generally fairly mature in terms of supply, product range and reach-even though reach in rural India still remains a challenge for the private sector and foreign banks. In terms of quality of assets and capital adequacy, Indian banks are considered to have clean, strong and transparent balance sheets relative to other banks in comparable economies in its region. The Reserve Bank of India is an autonomous body, with minimal pressure from the government. With the growth in the Indian economy expected to be strong for quite some time-especially in its services sector-the demand for banking services, especially retail banking, mortgages and investment services are expected to be strong. In recent years critics have charged that the non-government owned banks are too aggressive in their loan recovery efforts in connexion with housing, vehicle and personal loans. There are press reports that the banks' loan recovery efforts have driven defaulting borrowers to suicide. The IT revolution has had a great impact on the Indian banking system. The use of computers has led to the introduction of online banking in India. The use of computers in the banking sector in India has increased many folds after the economic liberalisation of 1991 as the country's banking sector has been exposed to the world's market. Indian banks were finding it difficult to compete with the international banks in terms of customer service, without the use of information technology. The RBI set up a number of committees to define and co-ordinate banking technology.

Bank Performance in India for the year ending 31.03.2013

	All Scheduled Commercial Banks	Public Sector Banks	New Private Sector Banks	Old Private Sector Banks	Foreign Banks
Number	89	26	7	13	43
Offices	92,114	75,779	9,718	6,283	334
Employees	10,96,984	8,01,659	2,03,733	66,208	25,384
Business Per Employee (₹Cr.)	12.1	12.7	9.3	9.72	21.7
Profit per Employee	0.08	0.06	0.12	0.08	0.46
Net Interest Margin (%)	2.79	2.57	3.3	2.94	3.89
Return on Equity (%)	13.84	13.24	16.51	16.22	11.52
Return on Asset (%)	1.03	0.78	1.74	1.26	1.94
Net NPA Ratio (%)	1.68	2.02	0.45	0.77	1.01
Capital Adequacy Ratio (%)	13.88	12.38	17.52	13.73	17.88

Source: Banking Annual December 2013

The total number of scheduled banks in India is 89 in which where maximum employees are working as on March ending 2013. The profit per employee is largest in Foreign Banks followed by New Private Sector Banks. Total numbers of ATMs installed in India by various banks as on end June 2013 is 1, 14,014. The maximum ATMs are for State Bank of India followed by New Private Sector Banks. While off site is highest for the Nationalised banks of India.

ATMs of Scheduled Commercial Banks in India for the year ending 31.03.2013

Bank type	On-site ATMs	Off-site ATMs	Total ATMs
Nationalised banks	55,760	58,254	1,14,014
State Bank of India	18,708	13,883	32,591
Old private sector banks	4,054	3,512	7,566
New private sector banks	15,236	27,865	43,101
Foreign banks	283	978	1,261

Source: http://www.rbi.org.in/scripts/Publications

Challenges and Opportunities in Banking Sector Reforms

Banking business in Indian is getting redefined it is faced with myriad challenges and opportunities, especially beyond 2009 when they would be fully exposed to competition. Banks in India are bracing themselves to be ready through adoption of newer technology strengthening their capital base to survive in the competitive environment, Reducing their NPAs, Bringing down operating costs, enhancing corporate governance and alignments, undertaking organizational restructuring and sharpening their customer-centric initiatives. Consolidation of merger and acquisition rout to effective compete with large global banks may not be far off, when viewed against such preparedness and positive signs from regulators. Technology is clear a prerequisite for growth and scale. Some of the challenges banks are facing today are as under:

- Changing needs of customers.
- Coping with regulatory reforms.
- Thinning spread.
- Maintaining high quality assets.
- Management of impaired assets.
- Keeping pace with technology up gradations.
- Sustaining healthy bottom lines and increasing shareholder value.

Conclusion

To accomplish total globalization, a common currency must be established which will ease the entry of foreign banks into domestic markets that can contribute to more efficiency through increased competition. In the other hand, a currency crisis in an emerging market would exaggerate this situation. Domestic borrowers, including banks, that obtain funds from abroad, usually borrow in a foreign currency such as the dollar to give foreign investors some reassurance about the value of their investments. The effect of financial globalization, therefore, on domestic financial fragility is not simple. Foreign direct investment both lowers the incidence of banking crises and shortens its duration. Overall the Indian banking sector is stronger and healthier today than it was a decade ago. The recent focus of some of the banks on micro finance and lending to SME firms are welcome changes both for the banking sector as well as the economy and society as a whole. Finding opportunities at the bottom of the pyramid rather than regulator loan-pushing is likely to help better distribution of the economic gains as well as opportunities. Managing the risk in banking through the implementation of global standards to be an important step for Indian banking sector in the coming year. Banks and financial institution will continue to experiment with new technologies and electronic, information based services to serve their customers better. The potential is great, yet the return on investment will be realized only in the long-term. Proper alignment of technology strategies with business goals will only ensure commensurate value addition to banks. Also banks are rediscovering the need for more brick and mortar branches as the most effective touch points for building relationships, marketing and selling. Technology advances like data mining and business intelligence will enable and empower branch personnel to realize higher customer life cycle value. The information-intensive nature of banking and financial services is unlikely to change. Banks will continue to find newer and innovative ways to put technology to their customers 'best use and will have to manage technology and business risks associated with these investments proactively.

Refernces

Beck, U. (2001). Living your life in a runaway world: individualization, globalization and politics.

Gray, J. (2002). False dawn. The delusions of global capitalism, London: Granta.

Khan M Y (1987), "Financial Services" Tata McGraw Hills, New Delhi

Pandey I.M. (1991), "Financial Management", Vikas Publishing House, New Delhi

Robertson, R. (1992). Globalization: Social theory and global culture. London: Sage.

World Bank, World Development Report 2000/2001: Attacking Poverty. (New York: Oxford University Press, 2001), p. 276 and p. 280. Telephone estimate from Financial Times

www.capitalmarket.com

www.economywatch.com

Chartered Financial Analyst

Business Standard – Banking Annual

A Comparative Analysis of The Quality of Services in Public and Private Sector Banks—A Case Study of Shimla Town

Vineeta

Research Scholar, Department of Commerce,
Himachal Pradesh University, Summer Hill, Shimla

Pallavi Berry

Research Scholar, Department of Commerce,
Himachal Pradesh University, Summer Hill, Shimla

Abstract

In the competitive era, quality of services is mandatory to attract customers. Banking institutions are facing challenge of the involvement of more and more institutions in the private sector that are providing a variety of services to the customers. Consequently, all banking institutions have to focus upon the service quality to sustain in the market. Banking system is an important constituent of overall economic system. In what measures a given banking system contributes to economic development depends upon the governing policy. The importance of banking institutions is felt rather deeply in the underdeveloped economies in the sense that these economies are usually short of capital and the task of mobilization of resources and their channelization to the priority sector belongs to such institutions. As quality of customer services is the basic requirement of any organization. Modern economy cannot function efficiently unless banking institutions work well. In this paper, attempt has been made to identify the variety of services provided by public and private sector banks and also a comparison has been made to determine the quality of services offered by both categories of the banking institutions.

Keywords: Banking System, Quality of services

Introduction

Banking system is an import constituent of overall economic system. In what measures a given banking system contributes to economic development depends upon the governing policy. Economies have expressed a wide variety of opinions on the effectiveness of banking system in promoting as facilitating economic development. Schumpeter, the 1st modern economist to study the relationship, regarding banking system as one of the two key agents (The other being entrepreneurship) in the whole process of development banks are considered to be the most important of all the financial intermediaries in financial system of a country.[1] The commercial banks can create credit on the bases of a fractional reserve system wherein a part of deposits are kept with central bank. Thus banks not only occupy an important place in economic structure of a country, but also plays an effective role in its economic growth.[2] In fact banking is the life blood of the modern commerce. It may truly be said that modern commerce is so dependent upon banking that any cessation of banking activities, even for a day or two, would completely paralyse the life of a nation. The importance of banking institutions is felt rather deeply in the underdeveloped economies in the sense that these economies are usually short of capital and the task of mobilization of resources and their channelization to the priority sector belongs to such institution. In a few countries, banks were created by the Government to exploit mineral resources and to build power plants on behalf of the Government, to draw up and carry out a general plan, to promote production in all sectors of economy, to obtain credit from abroad, to provide long term finance to private industry. Being a developing economy, India has all the features of such economy like preponderance of the agrarian sector, high density of population, low level of income, low standard of living and high propensity of consume low level of income. Low income leads to low saving which in turn, result in low capital formation. The economy, therefore, suffers typically from the vicious circle of poverty. Therefore, any effort to develop the economy requires an action to increase, mobilize and appropriately channelize the domestic financial resources towards productive investment in the economy. This calls for not merely the presence but also an active role of banking and other financial institutions.

Narasimhan and Thampy (2002)[3] in their paper have evaluated that in today's banking industry competition is rising very fast, to meet such competitions, firms need to develop appropriate strategies. **Kumar and Verma (2003)**[4] studied about the technical efficiency, benchmarks, targets for Indian public sector banks using Data Envelopment Analysis. **Krishnaveni and Prabha (2004)**[5] stated that service quality; service delivery and customer delight are probably the most debatable issues gripping the banking industry of our country. **Godse (2005)**[6] studied that the new delivery channels and improved access to customers information have changed the equation between the banks and customers. Tele-banking is a well known example in this regard and concluded that in the new era of online interaction, the direct access to account information has more or less resolved the customer concerns both on speed and accuracy. **Pushpaganthan (2006)**[7] examine the quality of customer services rendered by public, private and foreign sector banks with respect to promptness in rendering services, attitude of bank employees towards customers. **Kumar (2009)**[8] observed that although customer relationship management was supposed to transform business, its impact in India was mixed. It has been called strategic tool that combines business processes, technology, employees and information across an enterprise to attract and retain profitable customer. **Kamath (2010)**[9] evaluated the crucial factors which affects the customer satisfaction in Banks. SERVQUAL is measured on five different dimensions of tangibility, reliability, responsiveness, assurance and empathy. **Aggarwal (2011)**[10] compared the performance of PSB's with their private sector counterparts. He concluded that PSB's have lower capital adequacy than private banks, but the asset quality of PSB's is superior to private sector banks.

Need of The Study

The study of customer service quality of commercial banks especially public and private sector banks is a need based study in a fast changing scenario of the economy. In this study, it was felt that collecting views of bank customers will be helpful in indicating the directions in which the banks should move and restructured themselves to keep pace with time with reference to the quality of their customer services. Thus, it is high time for the banks to look inside themselves and see whether they are well equipped to meet the challenges of the economy. One way to do so is to find out the opinion of the customers and take suitable steps for better performance. The study was confined to the people in Shimla town only, so that intensive study could be done. Data was collected during the year 2012. Due to the limitation of time, money and other sources, a sample of 150 respondents has selected from various public and private sector banks in Shimla town and questionnaires were distributed among them.

Objectives of The Study

- To compare the quality of services offered by public sector banks and private sector banks.
- To study the level of satisfaction of customers regarding quality of customer services.

Research Methodology

The collection of information has been based on primary probe. The primary data were collected from customers of public and private sector banks with the help of questionnaire and scheduling.

Sample Size and Sampling Method

The sample size of the present study included 150 respondents of public and private sector banks of Shimla town. Out of 150 respondents 90 respondents from public sector banks i.e. SBI, PNB, UCO, UBI and Allahabad bank and 60 respondents from private sector banks i.e. HDFC, ICICI and AXIS banks have been selected. The respondents have been selected on Quota, Purposive and Convenience basis. In quota sampling quotas are set up according to some specified characteristics and in convenience sampling sample is obtained by selecting 'convenient' population unit.

Analysis and Interpretation

1) Arithmetic Mean
2) Standard Deviation
3) Coefficient of Skewness

Analysis & Discussion

Opinion about facilities provided to maintain general environment of Bank

The basic facilities like drinking water, toilet, parking facilities, waiting lodge, telephone facilities, privacy, suggestion box, fan cooler etc. holds very important place in both sector banks to maintain their general environment. Most of the customers prefer those banks which provide better services to its customers. The responses of the respondents with regard to these facilities are explained with the help of Table1 and Table 2.

Table 1 Opinion about facilities provided to maintain general environment of Bank

	Public Sector Banks					Private Sector Banks				
Statement	Mean	S.D.	Skew	Chi-Square	P. value	Mean	S.D.	Skew	Chi-Square	P. value
Drinking Water	3.4778	1.31737	-.494	11.222	.024	3.3500	1.38790	-.347	3.8333	.429
Toilet	3.3333	1.32394	-.284	5.778	.276	3.1333	1.33362	-.119	3.167	.530
Parking Facilities	3.3222	1.29674	-.309	6.778	.148	3.2667	1.32597	-.196	3.333	.504
Suggestion Box	3.3111	1.24200	-.365	11.889	.018	3.3833	1.26346	-.302	6.167	.187
Fan/ Cooler	3.6222	1.19529	-.640	22.111	.000	3.5000	1.14240	-.318	13.833	.008

Source: Primary Probe

Opinion of respondents with regard to facilities provided by public sector banks and private sector banks has been depicted in table 1. Some respondents expressed their opinion about basic facilities provided by banks to maintain general environment of bank is good; some have a view that facilities are average to the customers, some respondents have no opinion regarding these facilities, and some expressed their opinion about poor facilities. Both sector banks respondents having different opinion regarding these facilities. Table shows the opinion of the respondents with regard to drinking water, toilets, parking facilities, suggestion box, fan/cooler facilities, as the mean score of all these facilities in public sector banks are 3.4778, 3.3333, 3.3222, 3.3111, 3.6222 and in private sector banks are 3.3500, 3.1333, 3.2667, 3.3833, 3.5000 respectively, which shows the different opinion of the respondents of both sector banks. Further negative values of skewness indicate more concentration of opinion of respondents towards higher side on five point scale. Chi-square value of goodness of fit further supports the above finding.

Table 2 Opinion about the various facilities provided by Banks

	Public Sector Banks					Private Sector Banks				
Statement	Mean	S.D.	Skew	Chi-Square	P. value	Mean	S.D.	Skew	Chi-Square	P. value
Waiting Lodge	3.5778	1.31523	-.506	16.000	.003	3.4833	1.24181	-.455	9.000	.061

	Public Sector Banks					Private Sector Banks				
Statement	Mean	S.D.	Skew	Chi-Square	P. value	Mean	S.D.	Skew	Chi-Square	P. value
Telephone Facility	3.5000	1.39219	-.447	12.778	.012	3.4500	1.33309	-.400	6.167	.087
Working Space	3.5111	1.36772	-.401	14.667	.005	3.5167	1.37152	-.525	8.333	.080
Privacy	3.5444	1.34215	-.453	14.333	.006	3.5167	1.12734	-.557	21.333	.000

Source: Primary Probe

Opinion of the respondents with regard to facilities provided by public sector banks and private sector banks has been exhibited in table 2. It is observed that both banks respondents have different opinion towards these facilities. As the mean score of waiting lodge facilities in public sector banks is 3.5778 and mean score of private sector banks is 3.4833 respectively, which shows that respondents of public sector banks are more satisfied with this facility than that of private sector banks. Table shows the results of the opinion of the respondents of public and private sector banks towards telephone facility, as the mean score of both banks are 3.5000 and 3.4500 respectively. As far as for working space facilities, the mean score of public and private sector banks are 3.5111 and 3.5167 respectively. In the case of privacy, the mean score of public sector banks are 3.5444 and the mean score of private sector banks are 3.5167 respectively. The similar results are further supported by the highly significant value of chi-square which means that statistically there is significant difference in the distribution of opinion of respondents of both sector banks.

Table: 3

Opinion about time norms for services provided by Public and Private Sector Banks

	Public Sector Banks				Private Sector Banks			
Statement	Mean	S.D.	Skew	Chi-Square	Mean	S.D.	Skew	Chi-Square
Receipt of cash	4.0333	.79958	-1.005	89.444	3.6500	.70890	-.851	51.600
Issuance of Demand draft	3.4333	.79394	1.119	96.400	3.4000	.79119	.843	44.400
Deposit Receipt	3.4556	.98484	-.234	20.489	3.8333	.74029	-.240	32.267

	Public Sector Banks				Private Sector Banks			
Statement	Mean	S.D.	Skew	Chi-Square	Mean	S.D.	Skew	Chi-Square
Encashment of cheque through cashier	4.0889	.93189	-.436	31.156	4.5000	.77021	-1.151	30.000
Payment of demand draft	3.7667	.80797	-.200	33.289	3.7500	.77295	-.214	27.600
Payment of term deposit receipt	3.6222	.85562	.160	27.156	3.8833	.92226	.104	24.133
Updating of pass book	3.7889	.94208	-.469	20.489	4.2333	.92730	-1.018	26.933
Opening of a/c	2.9778	.73405	.035	7.267	2.6167	.61318	.448	19.300
Collection of local cheque	2.5556	.68877	.640	60.222	2.3667	.55132	.556	60.800
Collection of outside cheque	1.6667	.95987	1.109	69.378	1.6000	.97192	.682	56.000

Source: Primary Probe P. Value = .000

Present table shows the results of the opinion of the responses of the respondents about time norms for services provided by public and private sector banks. Table shows the mean score of public sector banks are much more than the mean score of the private sector banks, which means that respondents of public sector banks are much more satisfied than that of respondents of private sector banks regarding time norms. The negative value of the skewness the public and private sector banks indicate the contribution of opinion towards neutral side on five point scale. The chi square test of goodness of fit further supports the above finding that there is significant difference in the opinion of the responses of respondents of both sector banks with respect to time norms.

Attributes in Hi-Tech Banking

To exploit the full banking convenience internet banking, Mobile banking, ATMs, Electronic fund transfer, Demat account, and credit card services are offered by banks to its customers. So that they can avail anywhere, anytime access to number of diverse products and services under one roof. It is logical that these services and products are made available to attract large no of customers. In this table a comparison regarding these services being offered by both public and private sector banks is made.

Table 4

Attributes in Hi-Tech Banking

Public Sector Banks						Private Sector Banks				
Statement	Mean	S.D.	Skew	Chi-Square	P. value	Mean	S.D.	Skew	Chi-Square	P. value
Internet	3.5333	1.32563	-.503	13.000	.011	3.5500	1.26792	-.632	11.500	.021
Mobile	4.0111	.94208	-.682	22.800	.000	3.6333	1.37738	-.912	5.467	.141
ATM	3.8333	1.00839	-.696	9.822	.020	3.6333	1.43759	-.879	5.733	.125
Electronic Fund Trf.	3.9556	.98199	-.638	18.533	.000	3.5000	1.29536	-.629	11.167	.025
Debit/	3.6222	1.19529	-.640	22.111	.000	3.5000	1.14240	-.318	13.833	.008
Credit Card	3.2111	1.31110	-.249	5.222	.265	3.3667	1.31441	-.348	5.833	.212
Demat a/c	3.3778	1.32035	-.403	8.111	.088	3.4000	1.33022	-.381	5.833	.212

Source: Primary Probe

The opinion of the respondents of both sectors banks towards the internet, mobile, ATMs, electronic fund transfer, debit/credit card services and Demat a/c have been shown in above table. Mean score of Mobile, ATM, Internet, and Electronic Fund Transfer in public sector banks are more than that of private sector banks. It shows that respondents of public sector bank are using these services more, than that of the private sector. The negative value of skewness of the responses of the respondents of public and private sector banks indicate the contribution of opinion towards higher side on five point scale. Further, more or less significant value of chi-square in public sector banks shows that there is significant difference in responses of respondents regarding these services. And insignificant value of chi- square in private sector banks shows that there is more or less similar opinion of respondents. In case of debit/credit cards and Demat a/c Mean score of private sector banks is more than that of public sector banks, which shows more influence of these services in private sector banks. Further insignificant value of chi-square also shows that there is no significant difference in their opinion regarding these services in both sector banks.

Table: 5

Opinion of respondents toward overall services qualities of Banks

	Public sector Banks	Private sector Banks
Mean	3.8111	3.7333
Standard deviation	1.07989	1.10620
Skewness	-.434	-.259
Chi-square	7.689	5.067
P. value	.053	.167

Source: Primary Probe

Opinions of the customers towards overall service quality provided by public and private sector banks has been shown in table 5. It is observed from the result that the overall service quality of public sector bank is much better than private sector banks. As the mean score of public sector banks is 3.811 and the mean score of private sector banks is 3.7333 respectively. Further the negative value of skewness in case of both sector banks which shows the opinion of respondents towards higher side on five point scale. The standard deviation shows greater variation in private sector banks. The similar results are further supported by the highly significant value of chi square which means that statically there is significant difference in the distribution of opinion of respondents of public sector banks. In case of private sector banks chi-square is found insignificant which means that there is no significant difference in the distribution of opinion of respondents regarding overall service quality.

Table: 6 Measurement of attributes of customers regarding level of satisfaction in Public and Private Sector Banks

Public Sector Banks						Private Sector Banks				
Statement	Mean	S.D.	Skew	Chi-Square	P. value	Mean	S.D.	Skew	Chi-Square	P. value
The product and services provided are adequate	3.3889	1.31281	-.301	8.111	.088	2.6000	1.1960	.03197	14.833	.005
Services are provided promptly	3.3111	1.33782	-.304	5.444	.245	3.1167	.9930	.6184	12.933	.005
The staff are always willing to help	3.4222	1.34897	-.421	8.56	.073	3.1833	1.0968	-.0586	14.667	.005

Public Sector Banks						Private Sector Banks				
Statement	Mean	S.D.	Skew	Chi-Square	P. value	Mean	S.D.	Skew	Chi-Square	P. value
Electronic Fund Trf.	3.9556	.98199	-.638	18.533	.000	3.5000	1.29536	-.629	11.167	.025
Debit/	3.6222	1.19529	-.640	22.111	.000	3.5000	1.14240	-.318	13.833	.008
Credit Card	3.2111	1.31110	-.249	5.222	.265	3.3667	1.31441	-.348	5.833	.212
Demat a/c	3.3778	1.32035	-.403	8.111	.088	3.4000	1.33022	-.381	5.833	.212

In order to know the perception of the respondents regarding different type of services provided by public sector banks and private sector banks in Shimla town, a result of their opinion is given in table 6. The results show that the public sector banks respondents are more satisfied than that of private sector banks regarding these services. As the mean value of both banks are 3.3889 and 2.6000 respectively regarding the products and services provided are adequate, which shows the public sector banks has greater capability to satisfied its customers. In the case of services are provided promptly, the mean score of public sector banks is 3.3111 and mean score of private sector banks is 3.1167, which also shows that respondents of public sector banks are more satisfied than that of private sector banks. Chi-square value of goodness of fit furthers supports the above finding that there is significant difference in the opinion of the respondents of both sectors banks regarding level of satisfaction.

Conclusion and Suggestion

- It has been observed that convenient location, efficient and speedy services, reputed banks, longs working hours, are the main reasons for choosing the bank by customers. The study also shows that the majority of respondents prefer the public sector banks. The reason behind this is that the public sector banks have wide network of branches and ATM's than that of private sector banks in Shimla town. Therefore it is suggested that private sector banks should start campaign for creating confidence in the minds of customers.
- Public sector banks are offering qualitative services and products than that of private sector banks for meeting the needs of different target groups. The evaluation of Hi-tech

banking and personal banking services are considered very well in public sector banks as compared to private sector banks. So it is suggested that the banks will have to be on their toes all the time to understand the ever changing needs of the public. They should offer varied innovative and qualitative services to suit the convenience of the customers.

- Regarding ATM services and internet services it has been observed that majority of the respondents from public sector banks are satisfied with this service as compared to private sector banks in Shimla town. Since both type of banks are competing equally with each other, but private sector banks is little bit below the line in providing overall qualitative services when compared to public sector banks. It is suggested that ATMs should be facilitated with more security facilities.
- It is also found that there is problem of time norms; majority of respondents of public sector banks had their opinion that they receive cash, issuance of demand draft, payment of term deposit and collection of outside cheques within standard norms, but the respondents of private sector banks are not satisfied with these services. In respect of the completion of transactions within standard time fixed for it, private sector banks lag behind public sector banks.
- In order to face the competitive scenario effectively and to meet the customer's expectations, the bankers should draw up a strategic framework addressing the key issue concerning the quality aspects. There is need to educate the customers on the various aspects of banking.

References

1. Chawla A.S., "Nationalization and Growth of Indian Banking" Deep & Deep Publications, New Delhi, 1987, p.1.
2. Saggar Saveeta, "Commercial Banks in India", Deep and Deep Publications Pvt. Ltd., New Delhi- 27, 2005, p. 1.
3. Narasimhan M.S. and Thampy Ashok, "Activity based costing in banking service", Prajnan, Vol. XXXI, No. 2, 2002, pp. 95-102.

4. Kumar Sunil and Verma Satish, "Technical efficiency, benchmark and targets- A case study of Indian public sector banks", Prajnan, Vol. XXXI, No. 4, 2003, pp.275-299.
5. Krishanaveni R. and Prabha D. Divya, "Measuring service quality in banks-with special reference to Motor and pump industry", Prajnan, Vol. XXXIII, No. 1, 2004, pp. 47-54.
6. Godse Vasant, "Banker Customer Relationship", The Journal of Indian Institute of Banking and Finance, Vol. 76, No. 1, Jan-March, 2005.
7. Pushpangathan G., "A Study on the Quality of Customer Service in Public Sector Banks", Finance India, Vol. XX, No. 1, March 2006, pp. 209-211.
8. Kumar Pankaj, "Customer Relationship Management in Retail Banking", The Journal of Indian Institute of Banking and Finance, Vol. 80, No. 14, Oct-Dec. 2009.
9. Kamath OG Bharathi, "Measuring Service Quality (SERVQVAL) in Banks", Prajnan, Vol. XXXIX, No. 1, April-June 2010, pp. 41-51.
10. Aggarwal Pankaj K., "Performance of Public Sector Banks in the New Economy: A Comparison with Private Sector Banks", The Journal of Indian Institute of Banking and Finance, Vol. 82, No. 4, Oct-Dec. 2011, pp. 43-50.

New Industrial Policy On Industrial Performance

***Sanjay Kumar**

Research Scholar (Commerce), H.P University, Shimla-171005.

Abstract

Industrial policies are like booms which give a definite shape to industrialization through rules, policies, principles and procedures controlling industrial houses. It incorporates the fiscal policy, monetary policy, tariff policy and labour policy etc. Since the early eighties, various attempts have been made to liberalize the industrial policy framework. The new industrial policy of 1991 has wholly liberalized the industrial policy itself. The basic objectives of this policy were: Abolition of the Industrial licensing, Policy on Public Sector, Monopolistic and Restrictive Trade Practice limit and free entry to foreign investment and technology. Not only this, Industrial Location Policy is liberalized in addition to Abolition of Phased Manufacturing, Programmers for the New Projects and Removal of Mandatory Convertible Clause. The government has taken various initiatives for liberalizing foreign trade, currency transactions and to facilitate foreign direct investment inflows. These economic reforms have a great impact on the development of the industries. For further improvement, liberalization steps are introduced in every year's budget for improvement in industrial growth so that industries become more efficient and capable of facing global competition. This paper studies the impact of new industrial policy and new provisions on industrial performance.

Keywords: Industrialization, New Industrial Policy, liberalization, Industrial licensing

Introduction:

The stupendous revolution in information, communication and technology (ICT) are now reformulating the national boundaries and adjoining them with the global village. Today, even a down steam territory is wakened to face global competition. Indian economy, after the 1991 fiscal crisis, started to adopt the economic reforms with the objective of reviving the economy from slow growth to a market driven economy with optimum utilization of the resources. This was possible through rapid industrialization, therefore, it was considered necessary for reduction and abolition of poverty by providing employment, raising the standards of living of the peoples, improving the balance of payments and attaining self-reliability in the Indian economy. Therefore, small scale industrial sector provides assistance and regulates the market forces. The competition has widened the area in all directions i.e. not at national level but also at regional level. The basic objective of economic reforms was to improve productivity growth and competitiveness of Indian economy. The ultimate aim of these reforms were to make Indian industrial sector in general and small scale industrial sector in particular, more virtuous, upgraded with new technologies, with the assurance that these changes would make able this sector to achieve higher and sustainable growth both at national and regional level. Industry accounts for 26% of GDP and employs 22% of the total workforce. In the Post-liberalization era, the Indian private sector was faced competition not only in domestic state but also faced competition across the domestic boundaries. It was including the fear of cheaper Chinese imports. It has since handled the change by compressing costs, revamping management, and depending on cheap labour and new technology. However, this leads reduction in employment generation and increase in poverty and inflation.

Bala Subrahmanya (2004) highlighted the impact of globalization and domestic reforms on small-scale industries sector. The study stated that small industry had suffered in terms of growth of units, employment, output and exports. The Researcher highlighted that the policy changes had also thrown open new opportunities and markets for the small-scale industries sector. Bargal et al. (2009) examined the causal relationship among the three variables GDP, SSI output and SSI exports and also have compared the performance parameters of SSIs in the pre and post liberalization era. The study found that the annual average growth rate of different parameters of SSIs have declined in the period of nineties vis-à-vis the pre-reform years. There is an absence of any lead-lag causal relationship between exports and production in small-scale sector and GDP of Indian economy. Dixit and Pandey (2011) applied co-integration analysis to examine the causal relationship between SMEs output, exports, employment, number of SMEs and their fixed investment and India's GDP, total exports and employment (public and private) for the period 1973-74 to 2006-07. Their study revealed the positive causality between SMEs output and India's GDP. Singh et al. (2012) analyzed the performance of Small scale industry in India and focused on policy changes which have opened new opportunities for this sector. Their study concluded that SSI sector has made good progress in terms of number of SSI units, production & employment levels.

Objective of The Study

1. To study the provisions of new industrial policy.
2. To analyze performance of industrial sector in India.
3. To examine the impact of provision of new industrial policy on industrial performance.

Methodology:

The research is secondary in nature. Data has been collected from published sources and has been analyzed by applying percentage growth. Conclusions have been drawn and measures have been suggested.

ANALYSIS AND DISCUSSION: To achieve the objective of the research, analysis are drawn and discussed as under:

PROVISION UNDER NEW INDUSTRIAL POLICY: The year 1991 witnessed a drastic change in the industrial policy governing industrial development in the country since decades. This land mark changes which in the economic history of India in the form of Industrial Policy of 1991. The provisions of the new industrial policy are:-

1. Industrial licensing policy: - In a major move to liberalize the economy, the new industrial policy abolished all industrial licensing, irrespective of the level of investment, except for a short list of 18 industries related to the security and strategic ally was entirely a new chapter which was to enforce totally open economic system as compared to the earlier mixed system. The country decided to follow the lines of capitalism.
2. Policy on Public Sector: - The 1956 Resolution had reserved 17 industries for the public sector. The 1991 industrial policy reduced this number to 8 naming- Arms and ammunition; Atomic energy; Coal and lignite; Mineral oils; Mining of iron ore, manganese ore, chrome ore, gypsum, sulphur, gold and diamond; Mining of copper, lead, zinc, tin, molybdenum and wolfarm; Minerals specified in the schedule to the atomic energy (control of production and use order), 1953; and Rail transport. But later on five during these reserved industries under public sector were also dereserved. On May 9, 2001, the government opened up arms and ammunition sector also to the private sector.
3. Monopolistic and Restrictive Trade Practice limit: - Under the Monopolistic and Restrictive Trade Practice Act, all firms with assets above a certain size (Rs.100 crore since 1985) were classified as MRTP firms. Such firms were permitted to enter selected industries only and this also on a case by case approval basis. In addition to control through industrial

licensing, separate approvals were required by such large firms for any investment proposals. The New Industrial Policy therefore removes the threshold limit in assets in respect of MRTP companies and dominant undertakings. This eliminates the requirements of prior approval of the Central Government in respect of the activities concerning expansion, new undertakings etc. The MRTP Act has been accordingly amended. In the now amended Act, emphasis has shifted to taking appropriate action against monopolistic, restrictive and unfair trade practices on the part of monopolies.

4. Policy on Foreign investment and Technology agreements: - In the case of both foreign technology agreements sought by the Indian firms as well as foreign investment, it was necessary to obtain specific prior approval from the government for each project. It was argued that this caused undue delays and government interference and also hampered business decision making. The New Industrial Policy, therefore, prepared a specified list of high technology and high investment priority industries.
5. Abolition of Phased Manufacturing Programmes for New Projects: - In order to force the pace of indigenization in manufacturing sector, Phased Manufacturing Programmes have been in force in a number of engineering and electronic industries. The new policy abolished such programmes for future.
6. Removal of Mandatory Convertible Clause: - Since large part of industrial investment in India is finance by loans from banks and financial institutions, these institutions followed a mandatory practice of including a convertibility clause in their lending operations for new projects which provide them adoption of converting part of their loans into equity of felt necessary by their management. This has been interpreted as an unwarranted threat to the private firms to be taken over by the financial institutions. Hence, the new

industrial policy provided that financial institutions will not impose this mandatory convertible clause. Through the automatic route, subject to only SEBI (Securities and Exchange Board of India) regulations and sector specific caps on foreign direct investment; Existing companies with foreign direct investment are eligible for automatic route to undertake additional activities covered under automatic route; foreign direct investment up to 26 percent is eligible under automatic.

INDUSTRIAL PERFOMANCE:- The growth in the selected industrial sector is as under.-

Industrial Growth (%)

Sector	2007-08	2008-09	2009-10	2010-11	2011-12	2012-13	Apr-Jan 2012-13	Apr-Jan 2013-14
Coal	6.3	8.0	8.1	-0.2	1.3	4.3	6.5	1.0
Crude oil	0.4	-1.8	0.5	11.9	1.0	-0.6	-0.4	-0.3
Natural Gas	2.1	1.3	44.6	10.0	-8.9	-14.5	-13.6	-14.1
Refinery Products	6.5	3.0	-0.4	3.0	3.1	25.7	30.1	1.4
Fertilizers	-7.9	-3.9	12.7	0.0	0.4	-3.4	-4.0	2.5
Steel	6.8	1.9	6.0	13.2	10.3	3.3	3.3	4.1
Cement	8.1	7.2	10.5	4.5	6.7	7.7	8.1	3.4
Electricity	6.3	2.7	6.2	5.6	8.1	4.0	4.8	5.2
Overall index	5.2	2.8	6.6	6.6	5.0	5.8	6.9	2.4

Source: PIB, Ministry of Commerce and Industry, Index of Eight Core Industries,

Coal: Coal production declined by 0.7 % in January, 2014 over January, 2013. Its cumulative index during April to January, 2013-14 increased by 1.0 % over corresponding period of previous year. Crude Oil: Crude Oil production increased by 3.0 % in January, 2014 over January, 2013. The cumulative index of Crude Oil during April to January, 2013-14 declined by 0.3 % over the corresponding period of previous year. Natural Gas: The Natural Gas production declined by 5.2 % in January, 2014 over January, 2013. Its cumulative index during April to January, 2013-14 declined by 14.1 % over the corresponding period of previous year. Petroleum refinery production: Petroleum refinery production moderated by 4.5 % in January, 2014 over January, 2013. However, its cumulative index during April to January, 2013-14 increased by 1.4 % over the corresponding period of previous year. Fertilizers: - Fertilizer production registered a growth of 1.2 % in January, 2014 over January, 2013 and it registered a cumulative growth of 2.5 % during April to January, 2013-14 over the corresponding period of previous year. Steel: Steel production recorded a growth rate of 3.4 % in January, 2014 over January, 2013. The cumulative growth during April to January, 2013-14 was 4.1 % over the corresponding period of previous year. Cement: Cement production increased by 1.5 % in January, 2014 over January, 2013 and its cumulative growth during April to January, 2013-14 was 3.4 % over the corresponding period of previous year. Electricity: Electricity generation increased by 5.7 % in January, 2014 over the period of January, 2013 and it registered a cumulative growth of 5.2 % during April to January, 2013-14 over the corresponding period of previous year.

THE IMPACT OF NEW PROVISION ON INDUSTRIAL PERFORMANC

Industrial Production (In millions)

Out put	1950-51	1960-61	1970-71	1980-81	1990-91	2000-01	2008-09	2009-10	2010-11	2011-12
Food grains	50.8	82	108.4	129.6	176.4	196.8	234.4	218.1	244.5	257.4
Finished goods	1	2.4	4.6	6.8	13.5	32.3	63.4	96.1	76.3	82.8
Cement	2.7	8	14.3	18.6	48.8	99.2	187.6	207.1	216.7	230.5
Coal and lignite	32.3	55.2	76.3	119	225.5	332.6	525.2	566.1	570.4	583.1
Crude oil	0.3	0.5	6.8	10.5	33	32.4	33.5	33.7	37.7	38.1
Electricity generated	5	17	56	111	264	499	724	771	811	877
Plan outlay	260	1117	2524	15023	58369	185737	628161	717035	826268	1030461

Source: Economic survey 2012-13

The impact is the new provision of industrial policy on the performance of industries in India. In 1950-51 to 1990-91 increase in production in 25.6 million and after 1990-91 to

2011-12 in increase the 81 million. Then new industries policy is enhance the food grains production. But 1991 two decades in before and after is least production. This is 1970 to 1990 is 68 million increase but 1991 to 2010 is 41.7 million increase in production. Finished goods is 1950-51 to1990-91 increase 12.5 million and after 1990-91 to 2011-12 in 69.3 million increase. Cement industries is increase in 1950-51 to1990-91 46.1 million and 1990-91to 2011-12 increase 81.7 million. Coal and lignite is 93.2 in 1950 to 1991 and after 1991 increase are 357.6 million. Crude oil in 1950 to 1991 increases is 32.7 million and 1991 to 2012 increase in 5.1 million. But in two decades' before and after is least increase in a 0.7 increase in production. Electricity generated is 1950 to 1991 increase in 259 million and 1991 to 2012 is increase in 613 million production. The overall production increase excluding crude oil is very low production in India.

Conclusion and Suggestion

The industrial policies cover the procedures, principles, rules and regulations, which have inflate the industrial establishment of a country and shape the pattern of industrialization. The first industrial policy of the Government of India was announced in April 1948 and subsequently, industrial policy resolutions were announced in 1957, 1980, 1990 and 1991.The progress in industrial policy reforms enabled the country to pass through long but successful journey. At present, only five industries are having compulsory licensing. It has been concluded that the all the sector in increase the production but foods grains and crude oil is very less increase comparison before 1991. But electricity generated is very highly increased in production. The suggest that improvement of the food grains production and crude oil production.

Reference:

1. Rajan and zingales, 2003, saving capitalism from the capitalists, crown Business, New York.

2. Dr. Babita Thakur, Razika Gupta, Rajesh Singh, international Journal of scientific and research publication, volume-2, issue 12, Dec.2012.
3. Bala Subrahmanya, M.H. (2004), 'Small Industry and Globalization: Implications, Performance and Prospects', Economic and Political Weekly, Volume XXXIX, No.18, pp 1826-1834.
4. Bargal, H., Dashmishra, M., and Sharma, A. (2009), 'Performance Analysis of Small Scale Industries - A Study of Pre-liberalization and Post-liberalization period', International Journal of Business and Management, Vol 1, No 2.
5. Dixit, A. and Pandey, A.K. (2011), 'SMEs and Economic Growth in India: Cointegration Analysis', The IUP Journal of Financial Economics, Vol. IX, No. 2, PP. 41-59
6. Singh, R., Verma, O.P., and Anjum, B. (2012), 'Small Scale Industry: An Engine of Growth', Zenith International Journal of Business Economics & Management Research, Vol.2 Issue 5.
7. PIB, Ministry of commerce and industry, index of Eight Core industries, 31-01-2014.
8. Economic survey -2013.
9. RBI bulletin.

Banking Sector in India: an Overview

Sonika Asstt. Professor

Department of Commerce
Jawalaji Degree college Jawalamukhi (H P)

Abstract: It is by now well recognized that India is one of the fastest growing economies in the world. Evidence from across the world suggests that a sound and evolved banking system is required for sustained economic development. Banks plays an important role in the mobilization and allocation of resources in an economy. The sound financial position of a bank is the guarantee not only to its depositors but equally important for the whole economy of the nation.

Today the Indian banking system is among the best in the world because Indian banks are favorable on growth, asset quality and profitability; RBI and Government have made some notable changes in policies and regulation to help strengthen the sector India has a better banking system in place vis a vis other developing countries, but there are several issues that need to be ironed out. India's banking industry is at a watershed. Since 1991, India has been engaged in banking sector reforms aimed at increasing the profitability and efficiency of the 27 public-sector banks that controlled about 90% of all deposits, assets and credit. The banking sector, which was one of the most protected sector for five decades in the country and more precisely the public sector. However, some changes have been induced with a view to develop sound and efficient banking sector in India, at par improve the short-term risk perception but focus must rest on key structural changes that have to occur if Indian banking is to be a positive force and not a drag on the rest of the economy. It has met and successfully overcome several challenges over the last decade. But bigger challenges lie ahead. Present paper is an attempt to analyze various issues related to banking sector in India.

Introduction

In recent time, we has witnessed that the World Economy is passing through some Intricate circumstances as bankruptcy of banking & financial institutions, debt crisis in major economies the world and euro zone crisis. The scenario has become very uncertain causing recession in major economies like US and Europe. This poses some serious questions about the survival, growth and maintaining the sustainable development.

However, amidst all this turmoil India's Banking Industry has been amongst the few to maintain resilience. The tempo of development for the Indian banking industry has been remarkable over the past decade. It is evident from the higher pace of credit expansion, expanding profitability and productivity similar to banks in developed markets, lower incidence of non- performing assets and focus on financial inclusion have contributed to making Indian banking vibrant and strong. Indian banks have begun to revise their growth approach and re-evaluate the prospects on hand to keep the economy rolling.

Banking in India originated in the last decades of the 18th century. The Reserve Bank of India, India's central banking authority, was established in April 1935, but was nationalized on January 1, 1949 under the terms of the Reserve Bank of India (Transfer to Public Ownership) Act, 1948 (RBI, 2005b).

Banking Industry in India functions under the sunshade of Reserve Bank of India - the regulatory central bank. Banking Industry mainly consists of :

- Commercial Banks
- Co-operative Banks

The commercial banking structure in India consists of: Scheduled Commercial Banks

Unscheduled Bank. Scheduled commercial Banks constitute those banks which have been included in the Second Schedule of Reserve Bank of India (RBI) Act, 1934. For the purpose of assessment of performance of banks, the Reserve Bank of India categories them as public sector banks, and new private sector banks

Role of Banks

Banks play a positive role in economic development of a country as repositories of community's savings and as purveyors of credit. Indian Banking has aided the economic development during the last fifty years in an effective way. The banking sector has shown a remarkable responsiveness to the needs of planned economy. It has brought about a considerable progress in its efforts at deposit mobilization and has taken a number of measures in the recent past for accelerating the rate of growth of deposits. As recourse to this, the commercial banks opened branches in urban, semi-urban and rural areas and have introduced a number of attractive schemes to foster economic development.

Mobilization of resources forms an integral part of the development process in India. In this process of mobilization, banks are at a great advantage, chiefly because of their network of branches in the country.

Growth drivers of the Indian Banking Industry

High growth of Indian Economy : The growth of the banking industry is closely linked with the growth of the overall economy. India is one of the fastest growing economies in the world and is set to remain on that path for many years to come.

Rising per capita income : The rising per capita income will drive the growth of retail credit. Indians have a conservative outlook towards credit except for housing and other necessities.

New channel : Mobile banking is expected to become the second largest channel for banking after ATMs: During the last decade, banking through ATMs and internet has shown a tremendous growth, which is still in the growth phase. After ATMs, mobile banking is expected to give another push to this industry growth in a big way, with the help of new 3G and smart phone technology (mobile usage has grown tremendously over the years).

Objectives

1) To make an account of evolution of banking in India.
2) To study the impact of Nonperforming Assets on Indian banking sector.
3) To study are Indian Banking Sector are able to accept the Basel norms.

Phases of Indian Banking Sector

India cannot have a healthy economy without a sound and effective banking system. In the past three decades, India's banking system has earned several outstanding achievements to its credit. The most striking is its extensive reach. It is no longer confined to metropolises or cities in India. In fact, Indian banking system has reached even to the remote corners of the country. This is one of the main aspects of India's growth story.

Phase I

The first bank in India, the General Bank of India, was set up in 1786. Bank of Hindustan and Bengal Bank followed. The East India Company established Bank of Bengal (1809), Bank of Bombay (1840), and Bank of Madras (1843) as independent units and called them Presidency banks. The Reserve Bank of India came in 1935. The savings bank facility provided by the Postal department was comparatively safer, and funds were largely given to traders.

Phase 2

The government took major initiatives in banking sector reforms after Independence. In 1955, it nationalized the Imperial Bank of India and started offering extensive banking facilities, especially in rural and semi-urban areas. The government constituted the State Bank of India to act as the principal agent of the RBI and to handle banking transactions of the Union government and state governments all over the country. In 1969, 14 commercial banks in the country were nationalized. In the second phase of banking sector reforms, seven more banks were nationalized in 1980.With this, 80 percent of the banking sector in India came under the government ownership.

Phase 3

This phase has introduced many more products and facilities in the banking sector as part of the reforms process. In 1991, under the chairmanship of M Narasimham, a committee was set up, which worked for the liberalization of banking practices. Now, the country is flooded with foreign banks and their ATM stations. Efforts are being put to give a satisfactory service to customers. Phone banking and net banking are introduced. The entire system became more convenient and swift. Time is given importance in all money transactions.

Non-performing assets

The best indicator of the health of the banking industry in a country is its level of NPAs. Given this fact, Indian banks seem to be better placed than they were in the past.

Meaning of NPA

An asset is classified as non-performing asset (NPAs) if dues in the form of principal and interest are not paid by the borrower for a period of 180 days.

Capital adequacy norms

A third and a key issue will be the introduction of Basle II capital adequacy norms. These will make two demands on banks. They will have to measure the risks they bear much better. For this they will need to overhaul their management information systems so that they have a clear and quantifiable idea of their risks.

Suggestions

Major steps taken to solve the problems of Non-Performing Assets in India :-

1. Debt Recovery Tribunals (DRTs)

Narasimham Committee Report I (1991) recommended the setting up of Special Tribunals to reduce the time required for settling cases. Accepting the recommendations, Debt Recovery Tribunals (DRTs) were established. There are 22 DRTs and 5 Debt Recovery Appellate Tribunals.This is insufficient to solve the problem all over the country (India).

2. Securitisation Act 2002

Securitisation and Reconstruction of Financial Assets and Enforcement of Security Interest Act 2002 is popularly known as Securitisation Act. This act enables the banks to issue notices to defaulters who have to pay the debts within 60 days. Once the notice is issued the borrower cannot sell or dispose the assets without the consent of the lender.

3. Lok Adalats

Lok Adalats have been found suitable for the recovery of small loans. According to RBI guidelines issued in 2001. They cover NPA up to Rs. 5 lakhs, both suit filed and non-suit filed are covered. Lok Adalats avoid the legal process.

4. Compromise Settlement

Compromise Settlement Scheme provides a simple mechanism for recovery of NPA. Compromise Settlement Scheme is applied to advances below Rs. 10 Crores. It covers suit filed cases and case spending with courts and DRTs (Debt Recovery Tribunals). Cases of Willful default and fraud were excluded.

5. Credit Information Bureau

A good information system is required to prevent loans from turning into a NPA. If a borrower is a defaulter to one bank, this information should be available to all banks so that they may avoid lending to him. A Credit Information Bureau can help by maintaining a data bank which can be assessed by all lending institutions.

Some other suggestions:-

- The act should be judiciously and selectively applied so that NPAs could be converted into performing assets.
- Compromise wherever possible and desirable should be resorted to as per bank's extent terms and conditions.
- Creation of additional benches and enhancing the capacity of DRT (debt recovery tribunal) can be rationalized and delays could be avoided.
- Segregation of the benches should be done in order to ensure that a flood of small cases do not retard the disposal of larger cases.
- In order to reduce the balance of NPAs, Bank should constantly review and monitor the accounts and the progress of the project for which the loan has been sanctioned.

Conclusion

In last few years, the falling interest rates, gave banks very little incentive to lend to projects, as the return did not compensate them for the risk involved. This led to the banks getting into the retail segment big time. It also led to a lot of banks playing it safe and putting in most of the deposits they collected into government bonds. The banking sector in India needs to tackle these challenges successfully to keep growing and strengthen the Indian financial system. The NPA is the root cause of the global financial crisis that we observed recently. The world is still trying to recover from the after-effects of the crisis. The problem of NPA has received considerable attention after the liberalisation of the financial sector in India. Accounting norms have been modified substantially and mechanisms are in place for reduction of bad loans India's economic slowdown and high interest rates have started to impact the health of the country's banks in no uncertain terms, as is reflected by the rise in non-performing assets (NPAs) levels. There has been a continuous decrease in the time period considered to declare a loan as non-performing. The continuous decrease in the time period is to bring the Indian banking norms at par with international norms. This move will certainly reduce the NPAs and in turn improve the asset quality of the banks.

The RBI took a few important steps to make the Indian Banking industry more robust and healthy. The banking sector in India needs to tackle these challenges successfully to keep growing and strengthen the Indian financial system. Furthermore, the interference of the central government with the functioning of PSBs should stop. A fresh autonomy package for public sector banks is in offing. The package seeks to provide a high degree of freedom to PSBs on operational matters. This seems to be the right way to go for PSBs. This includes de-regulation of savings rate, guidelines for new banking licenses and implementation of Basel Norm III which represents the growth of banking sector in India. The growth of the banking sector will be one of the most important inputs that shall go into making sure that India progresses and becomes a global economic super power.

References

[1] Shrieves, R. E. "The relationship between risk and capital in commercial banks". Journal of Banking & Finance, 16(2): 439–457, 1992.

[2] Wolgast, M. "M&As in the financial industry: A matter of concern for bank supervisors?"Journal of Financial Regulation and Compliance, 9(3): 225-236, 2001.

[3] Al-Tamimi, H. A. H and Al-Mazrooei, F. M. "Banks' risk management: A comparison study of UAE national and foreign banks". Journal of Risk Finance, 8(4): 394-409, 2007.

[4] Sensarma, R. and Jayadev, "Are bank stocks sensitive to risk management?" Journal of Risk Finance, 10(1): 7-22, M. 2009.

[5] Zhao, T., Casu, B. and Ferrari, A. "Deregulation and Productivity Growth: A Study of The Indian Commercial Banking Industry". International Journal of Busines Performance Management, 10(4): 318-343, 2008.

[6] Goyal, K. A. and Joshi, V. "Mergers in Banking Industry of India: Some Emerging Issues".Asian Journal of Business and Management Sciences, 1(2): 157-165, 2011a.

[7] Fernando, A. C. "Business Environment". Noida: Dorling Kindersley (India) Pvt. Ltd. (2011), pp. 549-553.

[8] Gelade, G. A. and Ivery, M. "The Impact of Human Resource Management and Work Climate on Organizational Performance". Personnel Psychology, 56(2): 383-404, 2003.

[9] Bartel, A. P. "Human Resource Management and Organizational Performance: Evidence from Retail Banking". Industrial and Labor Relations Review, 57(2): 181-203, 2004.

Impact of Microfinance on Empowerment of Women

O.C.Rana

Asstt. Professor cum Director (T&P)
Sri Sai University Palampur (H.P)
rana.oc@rediffmail.com

Abstract:- Microfinance refers to the provision of financial services such as small loans, small savings, micro insurance and funds transfer facilities extended to socially and economically poor and disadvantaged segments of the society to enable them to increase their income levels and improve standard of living. Women Empowerment refers to the creation of an environment, where women can make independent decisions on their personal development as well as shine as equals in the society. Women Empowerment is the manifestation of redistribution of power that challenges patriarchal ideology and the male dominance. It is the transformation of organizations that reinforces and perpetuates gender discrimination.

The current research paper is the outcome of literature review, primary and secondary studies as regards the microfinance and women empowerment in the context of National Policy on Women Empowerment and as regards the recent programme initiated by the Banks and the Financial Institutions particularly in India.

The paper concludes that the provision of microfinance through financial services have certainly empowered the women to some extent as with microfinance, the women economic activities have enhanced resulting into increased women decisions to the financial matter. The increased household income under women control provides increased women control on income, assets and resources and increased access to markets. It has resulted into Women's Economic Empowerment which is resulting into household well-being and improvement in nutrition, health, literacy and happiness. With the women's economic growth, their place in society becomes more respectable resulting into women's Social and Political Empowerment ensuring protection in women's human rights. But women malnutrition, poor health, overwork, lack of education, mistreatment and discrimination are some of the issues to be looked into.

Keywords:- Microfinance, Women Empowerment, Economic Empowerment, Social Empowerment, Male dominance.

Introduction

In the simplest of words, Women Empowerment is basically the creation of an environment, where women can make independent decisions on their personal development as well as shine as equals in the society. In other words, Women Empowerment means the manifestation of redistribution of power that challenges patriarchal ideology and the male dominance. It is transformation of organizations that reinforces and perpetuates gender discrimination. The issue of empowerment of women is very complex and multidimensional. Pandit Jawaharlal Nehru has memorably said "You can tell the condition of a nation by looking at the condition of its women". In India, since the times of Nehru, the Government of India has made women empowerment a top priority. The welfare State of India advocates the responsibility of providing education, maternity, child welfare, protect and empower our women. The Government of India have believed in taking responsibility for implementing social programmes aimed specifically at women, particularly in terms of law enforcement, health and women's rights. The BJP is announcing that one third of all their positions will reserved for women to make them empowered. There is no doubt that the provision of microfinance and financial inclusions have certainly empowered the women to some extent, with Financial Services particularly the savings, credit, insurance and funds transfer facility, the women economic activities have enhanced resulting into increased woman decisions on the financial matters. The increased household income under women control provides increased women control on income, assets and resources and increased access to markets. This is certainly resulting into women's Economic Empowerment which is resulting into household well being and improvement in Nutrition, Health. Literacy and Happiness. With the women's economic growth, their place is society becomes more respectable resulting into women's social and Political Empowerment. There is protection in women's Human Rights.

The National Policy on Women Empowerment provides:

Legal Changes like inheritance, property, divorce and maintenance laws.

Decision making like power sharing, participation, women friendly personal policies.

Mainstreaming Gender policies, programmes, systems and strategies as women specific.

The Banks and the Financial Institutions have initiated many programmes and issues for Women Empowerment as: Women Development Cells, Gender Orientation, Training and Development, Credit, Services and Capacity Building, Women Consultative Committees, Women Specific Products, Women Entrepreneurship

But while observing the present conditions of the women in society, we observe that in India, more than 120 million women are very poor. India's maternal mortality rates in rural areas are among the world highest. India accounts for 19% of all lives births and 27% of all maternal deaths from the global perspective. Around 88% of pregnant women suffer from anemia. Every sixth infant death is due to gender discrimination. The Indian constitution grants women equal rights with men but in most

Indian families, a daughter is viewed as a liability and she is conditioned to believe that she is inferior and subordinate to men. The women malnutrition, poor health, overwork, lack of education, mistreatment and discrimination are still the bigger issues to be looked into. The empowerment of Indian women still appears a mirage.

Literature Review: There has been study on women's empowerment centering on microfinance programmes (Jayaweera, 1997). There has also been the study as access to credit automatically lead to women empowerment – while working on impact analysis of microfinance on women empowerment (Cheston and Kuhn, 2002), who pointed out that ability of women to be empowered through access to financial services depends on factors some linked to their individual situations and abilities and others dependent upon their environment and status of women as a group. The controlled capital, lack of access to information, social networks and other resources has been the inhibiting factors.

The study by Ramachandran (2002) reveals that credit, productive assets and skills cannot be used to empower the poor especially women unless they are aware, confident and powerful as collective to resist the landlords, moneylenders, unscrupulous middlemen and even development functionaries.

The study by Endeley (2001) showed that women having access income primarily ensures that Welfare of the family and can hardly address problems of women's oppression and subordination.

Hunt and Kasynathan (2001) advised that control on decision making regarding credit use, enterprises management, labour use, marketing and uses of income generated are the critical issues for understanding changes in gender relations and contribution of microfinance on women's empowerment.

Effective poverty targeting can ensure that short term, material benefits reach the poorest without necessarily leading to enhanced voice and equality (Rao, 2005)

The studies (Chaudhary, 2005; Garba, 1999; Gulati 1996 etc) have shown that access to microcredit and income cannot lead to the women empowerment unless associated with processes of changes in the power structure. Thus strategies for women empowerment could be different.

Objectives:

1) To examine the impact of microfinance on women empowerment.
2) To study various indicators like mobility, self confidence and capacity building, control over money earned by women's, say in decision making, women's autonomy and authority in women empowerment.
3) To study whether women empowerment is still a mirage.

Survey Analysis: Primary survey with the help of self designed questionnaire has been carried out in Bhawarna Block of district Kangra and responses from one hundred women pertaining to various Self Help Groups and Non Govt. Organizations selected at random has been carried out. The undernoted factors indicating the emerging women's empowerment have been covered and responses analyzed accordingly:

Women's Mobility: The change in mobility of women and social interactions are good indicators of women's empowerment. The microfinance has significant role in increasing the women's mobility. The survey covered responses from 100 women in this regard and undernoted responses obtained:

Women mobility frequency

	Generally	Occasionally	Never	Total
Visiting Hospitals	35	63	2	100
Visiting Local Markets	50	45	5	100
Visiting Parental Home	45	55	-	100

This shows that only 2% women for hospital needs and 5% women for marketing needs are dependent upon men. The women's movement is limited to 63% for hospital needs, 45% for market needs and 55% for visiting parental home as per occasionally response. The "never" and "occasionally" mobility still provides adequate scope for women mobility. However the responses under the "Generally" category to 35%, 50% and 45% extent show signs of improving women's empowerment.

Women's Confidence and Capacity Building: The microfinance is impacting the capacity building of women for financial management by savings, loans, insurances and easy funds transfers. This is increasing the women's confidence in family financial decisions and social participation. The undernoted responses were obtained on the basis of questionnaire survey:

Women's Confidence and Capacity Building

	Considerably	Marginally	Negligible	Total
Improved	43	37	3	83
NO Change	-	-	15	15
Deteriorating	-	-	2	2

83% of the respondents have observed improvement in confidence gained through microfinance capacity building, out of which 43% shown considerable, 37% as marginal and 3% as negligible improvement. The 15% responded have shown no change where as 2% as deteriorating position to negligible extent. Thus it is observed that microfinance is creating positive impacts to large extent in women's empowerment.

Control over money earned by women: Control over money earned by women, provides a degree of authority and sign of empowerment.

	Considerable	Marginally	Negligible	Total
Women Self	3	45	5	53
Husband	2	35	5	42
Father- in Law	-	-	2	2
Mother- in Law	-	-	3	3

It is observed in the survey that 53% of the women are having their own control over money earned by them in microfinance oriented schemes which is an excellent sign of empowerment. The husband control has been observed to 42% where as the control by father-in law is negligible.

Women's say in Decision – making: Women's participation in family decision – making is the significant indicator of women's empowerment. The provision of financial services to women is positively impacting their empowerment. It has been observed through survey that 25% of women are having considerable.

Women's say in decision making in family matters

Matter Concerning	Considerable	Marginal	Negligible	Total
Children education	25	66	9	100
Food consumption	35	60	5	100
Clothing	40	55	5	100
General matters including Social Participation	43	54	3	100

66 % as marginal and 9% as negligible say in family decision making as regards children education. As regards routine food family matter, the 35% of women have considerable say 60% as marginal and 5% as negligible say. In clothing matters 40% women have considerable, 55% as marginal and 5% as negligible say in the family. In general matters including social participation 43% of the women have considerable, 54% as marginal and 3% as negligible say in the family. The higher say of women in family matters is an excellent sign of women's empowerment.

Women's Autonomy and Authority: The autonomy is the capacity to manipulate one's personal environment. It is s multidimensional concept and difficult to measure. It has been tried to understand the level of authority achieved through autonomy as achieved by joining Self Help Groups and availing microfinance.

Authority Index

	Husband	Wife	Joint	Total
Children Education	27	25	48	100
Family Expenditure	33	27	40	100

	Husband	Wife	Joint	Total
Medical treatment	30	25	45	100
Social participation	25	32	43	100
Political participation	35	21	44	100

The survey reveals that the women's autonomy and authority as regards the children education is 25%, in family expenditure as 27%, in medical treatment and family welfare as 25%, social and religious functions participation as 32% and political participation as 21% in the family besides the Joint say which commands an excellent autonomy and authority showing the women's empowerment as result of microfinance awareness.

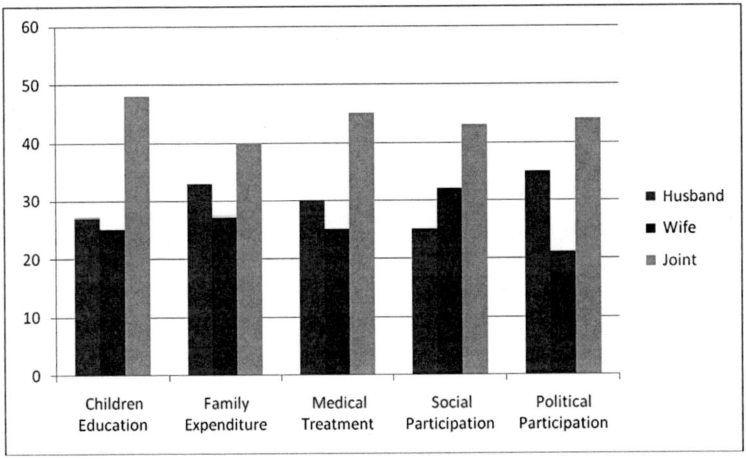

Conclusion:

It has been observed from the analysis of data obtained from survey that microfinance is impacting the women's empowerment to considerable extent. The self Help Groups are becoming successful in reducing the poverty, increasing the income and empowering the women particularly in rural areas.

Microfinance is helping in reducing the poverty and increasing the self employment opportunities. The increased income of the women is resulting into women's empowerment. The increased mobility and participation in the social and religious affairs in the society is resulting to women's social empowerment. The women are also participating in the politics thereby resulting into the women's political empowerment. Although the results are encouraging, yet much has to be done to fully ensure the women empowerment.

References:

BIRD (2009), "The microfinance Review," Journal of the centre for Microfinance Research.

IBA (2006), "Indian Banker," monthly Journal.

Micro Financing : A Blessing for The Poor

Ms.Neetika Sharma

Asstt.Prof.in commerce
GGDSD College Rajpur(Palampur)
Email: nitikakatochplp@gmail.com

Abstract: The responsibility of meeting the credit needs in the rural areas of India was entrusted primarily with the cooperative sector and later to the commercial sector. One of the major objective of nationalization of major commercial banks was to improve the flow of formal institutional credit to rural households. The need for microfinance in India has arisen due to failure of formal banking system in meeting the credit needs of millions of rural and urban people. The micro finance is widely used to refer to institutions governing savings, credit, insurance and monetary payment by relating poor people , including those regulated by both official laws and informal norms. Analysis of micro-finance is widely framed as a purely micro issue, contested on the motivation and behaviour of specific users and providers. In India private microfinance organizations is viewed positively as a force for promoting financial inclusions by "making markets work for the poor."Micro finance is a program for the poor and by the poor to mobilize the savings and use them to meet their financing needs. The role of micro finance as the most suitable and feasible alternative in accomplishing the goals of growth and poverty alleviation.

Keywords: micro-finance, micro-credit.

Introduction

The term microfinance originally described the provisions of very small loans, so called "Micro-Credit "to the poorer parts of the population in order to help them engaging in productive activities and moving out of poverty. Over time, microfinance has broadened its agenda and has included other financial services, such as savings or insurance. At the first Microfinance program evolved in the mid-1980s, Microfinance is a quite recent phenomenon. Consultative group of Assist the Poor (CGAP) defines microfinance as "the supply of loans, savings and other basic financial services to the poor". Financial services of microfinance usually involves small amount of money (loan, savingsetc.)Therefore,theterm microfinance helps to differentiate these services from those which formal banks provide. On the supply side of microfinance, there are whole sort of institutions generally known as Microfinance Institutions (MFIs).These institutions include local, national and international, nonprofit, governmental and non-governmental organizations, plus microfinance specialized banks and other commercial banks. These institutions (MFIs) provide a microfinance service that is small loans to poor borrowers. The idea of micro finance started in the 1950s when the government and various donor organizations started providing subsidized agricultural credits to small farmers. During 1980s attention shifted to women small entrepreneur such that they could establish their small business and therefore raise their household income and welfare. During these times there emerged various non-governmental organization (NGOs) specializing in providing loans to poor. In 1990s these NGOs turned themselves into formal financial institutions now known as MFIs.

Need of The Study

Microfinance is the provision of financial services to people who wouldn't usually qualify for traditional banking services because they have no form of collateral or formal identification. A loan as small as can help someone living in poverty start or grow their own small business. This enables them to earn an income so they no longer have to struggle to afford food, clean water, healthcare and an education for their children.

Objectives

- To Study the conceptual framework of microfinance.
- To study the role of micro finance in poverty alleviation and women empowerment.

Methodology

Secondary sources of data are used. Data published by various institutions such as Government of India, World Bank, Consultative Group to Assist The Poor (CGAP), Reserve Bank of India(RBI),National Bank for Agriculture and Rural Development (NABARD),State Level Bankers Committee (SLBC), etc.

Analysis & Interpretation

The basic idea of microfinance is that poor people are ready and are willing to pull themselves out of poverty if given access to economic inputs. Micro-credit programmers offer a combination of services and resources to their clients in addition to usual credit for self-employment. Microfinance services are also enhancing women's capabilities, which can make significant differences to overall development of women.

- **How Microfinance works...**

By helping a mother buy a sewing machine to start a tailoring business or a father buy seeds to plant a vegetable garden, small loans enable people in poverty to earn an income and provide for their families. As each business grows, loans are paid back and lent out again. With 97% of loans repaid, the cycle continues, year after year. Each successful business can feed a family, employ more people and eventually help empowered a whole community.

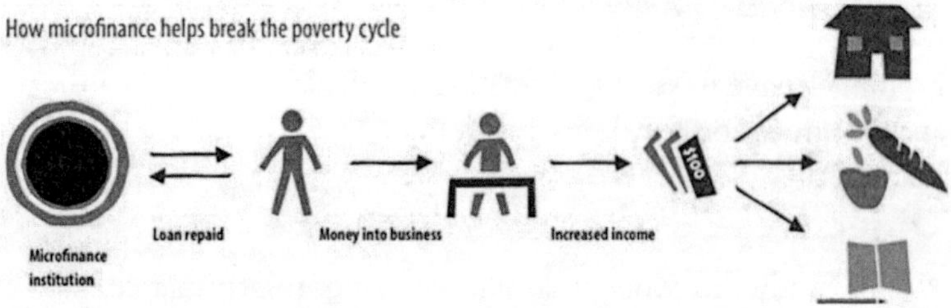

More than loans

As well as small loans (or micro credit/micro loans) microfinance also includes:

- Savings accounts to help provide a safety net in times of need and help with planning for the future
- Micro insurance to protect against emergencies and disasters
- Micro pensions to help provide an income in old age
- Fund transfers and remittance products to help families living far apart access their incomes.
- Non-financial services such as business development to strengthen enterprises, and financial literacy training to empower families to look after their own finances.

Beyond this, access to these kinds of services helps empower families to become active participants in society, building self-confidence and dignity.

- **Poverty Alleviation**

The lesson learnt from the experience of development finance so far is that poor people have often been excluded from financial services due to their inability to provide adequate collateral. This exclusion drives them into the informal financial sector in order to get access to credit. In many developing countries this sector is dominated by local moneylenders who are imposing very high interest rates that are often serviced by bonded labor while the debt itself is passed from generation to generation. Consequently, the provision of official financial services has been an important tool for poverty alleviation in the development strategies since the 1970s, initially through the government-directed credit programs and later through Microfinance. Given the widespread application of credit provision as a tool for poverty alleviation, it is important to understand why and in what context credit provision can influence the livelihood of the poor. In general, two dimensions of poverty can be distinguished, namely the income dimension and the participation dimension. The former is an exclusive material dimension and is generally measured by annual household income. The policy objective in the context of this poverty dimension is to lift poor households from below the poverty line above it. The participation dimension on the other hand, moves beyond a material definition of poverty and takes a broader view on poverty, comprising many forms of deprivation that poor people experience, such as social inferiority, powerlessness, humiliation and isolation. The World Development Report 2000/2001, dedicated to global poverty, identified two ways by which the provision of financial services in general and Microfinance in particular can have an impact on poverty. Firstly, Microfinance can strengthen poor people's economic activities by making investment in assets more affordable and thus allowing them to engage in profitable business opportunities. This is called the income-generating effect. The second effect of Microfinance, the vulnerability effect, is based on the assumption that the availability of financial services can help to improve poor households' risk management and reduce their vulnerabilities in the face of economic shocks such as illness, income volatility, price fluctuations or natural disasters. Even though both of these ways are trying to reduce income-related poverty, they are two different approaches. The income-generating effect aims at moving households from a stable "below poverty line situation" to a stable "above poverty line situation" by providing investment loans. The vulnerability effect, on the other hand, is understood as reducing the effects of income fluctuations or dramatic reductions in income by offering loans for emergency consumption or saving schemes. The desired impact of these approaches is illustrated below.

Diagram 1: Income-generating and vulnerability effect of Microfinance

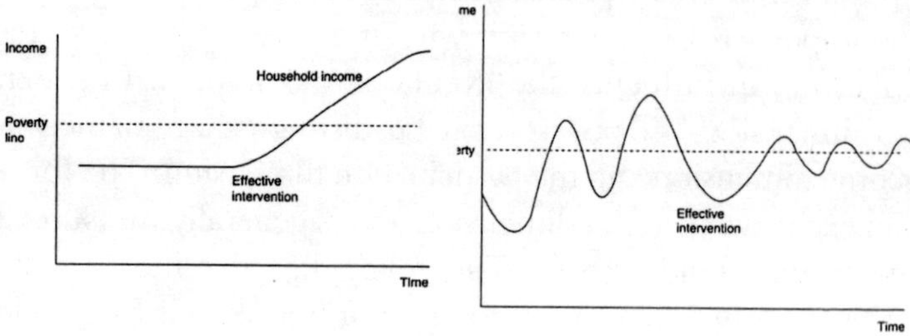

Income-generating effect Vulnerability effect

- **Empowerment of Women**

"Micro- credit plays a critical role in empowering women, helps

Deliver new found respect, independence and participation for women in their

Communities and in their households."

Juan Somavia, ILO
Director General

According to the two poverty dimensions of income and participation, the approach of Microfinance is underpinned by a broader definition of poverty alleviation, comprising as well non-material and social development objectives. In this context, women empowerment is one of the most commonly used impact indicators for Microfinance programs beside the income-related poverty dimension.15 This enhanced understanding of poverty alleviation is based on the evidence that poor people's lives are characterised by powerlessness and voicelessness limiting their opportunities and also complicating their interactions with employers, markets and other institutions. This in turn leads to lower self-confidence which is further increasing powerlessness and isolation. Empowerment is a strategy to break this vicious circle as it tries to promote sharing of control as well as entitlement and the ability to participate in decision making processes. The strategy of empowerment is particular targeted at women as they are disproportionately affected by poverty and lack of participation. The UN's Fourth World Conference on Women, which took place in Beijing in 1995, already articulated the objective of many Microfinance programs by demanding to "strengthen women's access to credit and capital on appropriate terms equal to those of men through scaling-up of institutions dedicated to promoting women's entrepreneurship".

Strategies for Advancing Gender Equality Through Microfinance

Strategies to facilitate positive impact on women form a basis for tailoring microfinance policies, practices and products to better address gender equality and promote women's empowerment.

- **Internal MFI gender mainstreaming,**

Crucial components of a proactive women's empowerment strategy include training on gender analysis for MFI staff members, the utilization of female loan officers and the provision of equal employment and management opportunities for women. MFIs should also incorporate empowerment indicators, such as the proportion of women clients in the loan and savings portfolio, into client monitoring and assessment processes.

- **Adjusting financial services to better address women's needs**

Microfinance products generate different outcomes for men and women. MFIs should therefore tailor product specifications, such as loan amounts and repayment schedules, to diverse client needs. Individual loan products designed for women are also important for enabling enterprise growth. Savings products designed for women are a fundamental element of risk management. A diversified MFI product offer should also include other financial services that help reduce vulnerability, such as micro insurance. Adjusting collateral requirements and encouraging the registration of property in women's names are other essential components of gendered microfinance.

- **Non-Financial Services**

Non-financial services with conditionalities to credit access, such as carefully designed adult literacy and business training programs, can facilitate women's access to better jobs and income-generating opportunities and are perhaps the most effective means of promoting gender equality.

- **External marketing for community awareness**

Marketing campaigns directed at women can positively influence both men and women's attitudes on women's status and employment in the community by helping male community members to accept economic opportunities for women, by building women's self-confidence and by facilitating community approval of women's projects.

- **Groups to strengthen women's networks**

MFI women's groups should be utilized to promote and strengthen women's networks and not merely as a means of lowering program costs. Women's groups are useful vehicles for non-financial service delivery, such as literacy and health programs. Groups also encourage linkages between women and other active community associations and the larger civil society network as a whole. and improved protection against illness and Sudden shocks. By opening up the schooling and training activities to girls and young women, the project helped break the generational transmission and feminization of poverty. Moreover, through microfinance, women previously excluded from the financial sector gained access to credit and effectively learned how to borrow, profit from, and repay loans.

- **Financial Sector Development**

While poverty orientated Microfinance understands the provision of financial services only as a means to achieve the main objective of poverty alleviation, the commercial approach to Microfinance regards the provision of sustainable financial services to low-income people as its main objective. The application of commercial principles and the emphasis of the private sector are seen as ways to develop an effective financial sector in areas that have been underserved so far. Accordingly, this approach is more concerned with the scale of outreach rather than with targeting the poor and the final impact on the borrower. A sufficient demand for credit and the repayment of the loans is regarded as evidence that Microfinance has served its purpose. This commercial approach is closely connected with the term of "New Wave Microfinance", which can be seen as a strand of the neo-liberal development approach dominant since the 1980s. Accordingly, this movement has also received significant support from the major development and donor institutions like the World Bank or the European Bank for Reconstruction and Development (EBRD) MFIs following certain "best practice" principles are likely to achieve financial sustainability and can therefore grow without constraints from subsidy-providing donors.s

Diagram 2.
Impact of Microfinance on different sectors of economy

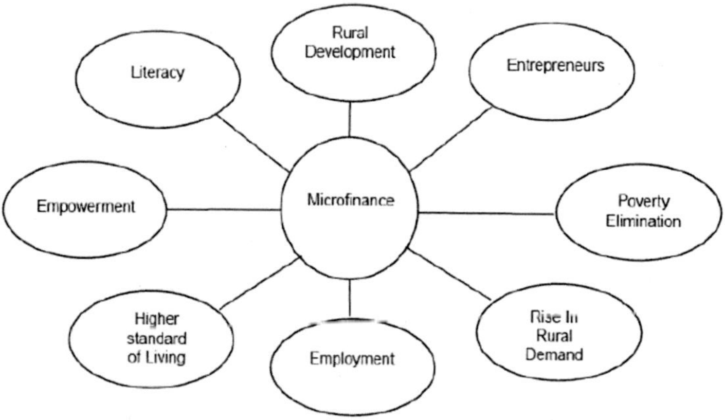

Conclusion

In India, Economic Reforms with a human face have been accepted as the guiding principle of sustainable development. Keeping the Poor at centre stage, the Policies need to be reoriented so as to develop and optimize the potential of such a large segment of the Population and enable them to contribute in the growth process significantly in terms of output, income, employment and consumption. After the pioneering efforts of the last ten years, the Micro Finance Scene in India has reached a take-off point. With some efforts substantial progress can be made in taking MFIs to the next orbit of significance and sustainability. This needs innovative and forward-looking policies, based on the ground realities of successful MFIs. This, combined with a commercial approach from the MFIs in making Micro Finance Financially Sustainable, will make this Sector vibrant and help achieve its single-minded mission of providing Financial Services to the Rural Poor. It is necessary to recognize that we, in India, have to focus on extending financial services in both rural and urban areas for ensuring financial inclusion of all segments of the population. At the same time, one should avoid the temptation of creating one set of banking and financial institutions to cater to the poor or the unorganized, and another for the rest. The medium to long-term objective should be to ensure inclusion of all segments in the mainstream institutions while taking advantage of the flexibility of multiplicity of models of delivering a wide range of financial services. In this light, a comprehensive framework to revive the cooperative credit system, revitalize the Regional Rural Banks and reorient commercial banking system needs to get a high priority while simultaneously encouraging and enabling the growth of micro-finance movement in India, which has been very successful. We need to build on its strengths and extend it to vast areas, which are inadequately covered by both banking and micro-credit entities. Micro-finance, broadly defined, needs to be explored in the light of the new paradigm described. RBI and NABARD recognize the growing importance of micro-finance and are committed to enable its healthy growth. However, several issues, both in regard to regulation as well as development of the MFIs need to be considered and must be comprehensively addressed. While the report of the Khan Committee would provide a good starting point for taking a view on developmental aspects, in particular, the CGAP's Guiding Principles on Regulation and Supervision on Micro-finance provide a valuable and globally relevant framework in regard to the regulatory issues. The proposed forum for a consultative process on the MFIs would also be useful in evolving an appropriate framework for development of the MFI sector. No doubt, a very well-crafted balance between the regulation and growth objectives would be warranted in formulating our approach to a regulatory regime, keeping in view the big challenge of financial inclusion of a large segment of the Indian population.

References

- Growth of Micro credit in India: An Evaluation (90th Conference Volume of Indian Economic Assiciation)2007
- MS,Gupta 2008 Micro Finance Through Self Help Groups (An Emerging Horizon for Rural Development Vol.61(3),The Indian Journal Of Commerce
- Choudhary Meenakshi,2013 International Journal of Business and Management Invention Vol.2PP72-76
- Pandey Manas2008 Microfinancing a blessing for poor, The Indian Journal Of CommerceVol.61(3)
- Jens Osthoff MA International Studies (International; Economic Management)University of Bisminghon
- Mehmood Ahmed 2009,Micro Financing:A burden or Blessing,Proceeding 2nd CBRC Lahore,Pakistan Nanjibhai D. ranparia
- Dr.Christabell.P.J., Vimal Raj.A 2012 Financial Inclusion in Rural India: The role of Microfinance as a tool Vol.2PP21-25 (IOSR Journal of humanties and Social Science)
- Dr.E.A.Parameswara Gupta ,K.G.Satheesha MicroFinance,Poverty Alleviation and Women Empowerment Vol.2 2013 (International Journal ofEntrepreneurship & Business Evviornment Perspectives)
- Mr.Nanjibhai D. Ranparia 2013 Financial Inclusion in Gujarat Vol.2 (International Journal of Scientific Research.
- CGAP,website http://http://www.cgap.ogr

- Ghildiyal,Vipin(2009) Microfinance and Poverty alleviation. (MERI Journal of Management and IT)
- RBI.Report of the Working Group To Review The Business Correspondent Model, Mumbai ,2009
- Government of India (GOI),Economic Survey 2009,New Delhi.

Devaluation of Rupee and its impact on Indian Economy

Ritesh Mahajan

School of Business Management ,Dept. of MBA,Dharamshala

E-mail: ritesh1122@yahoo.co.in

Abstract: Global economy is much more interlinked than it was earlier due to lot of trade taking place between different countries. It goes without saying that U.S. is major trading partner for many nations and biggest trading importer of goods and services from across the world. Change in any direction in U.S. economy is directly going to affect economy of all related countries. The outlook for the Indian currency (INR) has gone through a drastic change in the last few months. The Indian currency has depreciated by more than 20 percent since April 2008 and breached its crucial 69-level against the greenback on sustained dollar purchases by foreign banks and stronger dollar overseas. The fall in the value of Indian rupee has several consequences which could have mixed effects on Indian economy. In this research paper author tries to define the Rupee Devaluation, causes of devaluation, effect of FII's on Indian Rupee devaluation and tries to establish relationship between GDP and Rupee value during 2007 to 2013 fiscal years. The Research approach is exploratory during the current study and this paper attempts to find relationship between different variables which affects the Devaluation of INR with respect to foreign currencies majorly US Dollar. So this paper analyses the recent trends of devaluation of Indian rupees/ US Dollar for last six years and their impact on FII , GDP , Foreign Currency and we used Spears man rank correlation method for showing the relationship between above variables.

Keywords: Rupee Devaluation, FII, GDP, Foreign Currency.

Introduction:

Currency is the major source of transaction and value maintenance for its holder. The economy of any nation largely depends upon the value of its currency with respect to other international trading currencies. From the beginning of slowdown in Indian Economy during 2007 till now the Rupee exhibit greater volatility in term of value. The value of Rupee in 2008 nearly breached the Rs 50 per dollar mark and closed at 49.90 - it's weakest since May 14, 2009.The weakening of Indian rupee against other foreign currencies, especially dollar, is not good news for Indian government and importers. A depreciating rupee may compound the macroeconomic problems as prices of imported goods will surge and worsen the current account deficit. India won't be able to take advantage even if commodity prices ease due to global slowdown. The appreciating rupee is posing a unique set of challenges for the Indian economy. The impact would not be limited to macro economy alone but it will also affect down to the level of firms under various sections of economy. This is exploratory study based on Rupee Dollar relationship in terms of Rupee appreciation that is dollar depreciation and rupee depreciation that is dollar appreciation. It provides valuable insights into impact of changes in currency relations on various sectors of economy keeping in focus economy in general and Indian economy in particular. Pros and Cons of currency appreciation and depreciation are studied as boon and bane for the economic growth. It also provides suggestions or steps needed to control as well as to overcome ill-effects of excessive fluctuations between rupee and dollar keeping in view current trends.

Devaluation means a fall in the value of domestic currency in terms of foreign currency/currencies. Devaluation is a reduction in the value of a currency with respect to those goods, services or other monetary units with which that currency can be exchanged. A substantial drop in the value of a currency, relative to the price of gold or the currencies of other countries.

Types of Devaluation:

i) Market-Force Devaluation:- When exchange rate falls in floating exchange rate system due to free interaction of market forces, it is called depreciation. In simple words demand and supply of a currency in international market affect the currency rates. This could be in two ways:
   - When supply increases.
   - When demand decreases.

   (FLOATING EXCHANGE RATES)

ii) Planned devaluation

   The active decision of a government to reduce the value of its own currency vis a vis other currencies. Devaluation occurs exclusively in fixed currencies, when the currency in question is pegged to another

   (FIXED EXCHANGE RATES)

Historical Overview:

From 1950 to 1973 Indian rupee was linked to British pound. In 1966 and 1973 devaluation happened. On 24th September 1975, the connection between Indian rupee and pound was broken.

In 1975, the rupee ties to the pound sterling were disengaged. India established a float exchange regime. With the rupee's effective rate placed on a controlled, floating basis and linked to a "basket of currencies" of India's major trading partners.

In 1993 Liberalized exchange rate system (LERMS) was replaced by the unified exchange rate system and hence the system of market determined exchange rate was adopted. However, the RBI did not relinquish its right to intervene in the market to enable and control the Indian currency. Before 2011 India had faced two major devaluation that is in the year 1966 and 1991. So let's understand the reasons and the measures adopted by government for the major devaluations that took place in India.

The 1966 Devaluation:

As a developing economy, it is to be expected that India would import more than it exports. Despite government attempts to obtain a positive trade balance, India has had consistent balance of payments deficits since the 1950s. The 1966 devaluation was the result of the first major financial crisis the government faced.

Causes

a) Increasing trade deficit:

Despite government attempts to obtain a positive trade balance, India suffered a severe balance of payments deficits since the 1950s. Inflation had caused Indian prices to become much higher than world prices at the pre-devaluation exchange rate. When the exchange rate is fixed and a country experiences high inflation relative to other countries, that country's goods become more expensive and foreign goods become cheaper. Therefore, inflation tends to increase imports and decrease exports. Since 1950, India ran continued trade deficits that increased in magnitude in the 1960s.

b) India's war with Pakistan in late 1965:

The US and other countries friendly towards Pakistan, withdrew foreign aid to India, which further necessitated devaluation. Because of all these reasons, Government of India devalued Rupee by 36.5% against Dollar.

Steps taken by government

a) Imposed Quantitative Restrictions

The government used the method of QRs with varying levels of severity until the Import- Export Policy of 1985-1988. Periodically, when import prices reached a premium, the government would impose import tariffs in order to absorb the gains accruing to foreign exporters as a result of India's import

b) Provided export Subsidies

Government began to subsidize exports in an effort to further narrow its consistent current account

The 1991 Devaluation:

1991 is often cited as the year of economic reform in India. Surely, the government's economic

policies changed drastically in that year. Then the Import-Export Policy of 1985-1988 replaced

import quotas with tariffs. This represented a major overhaul of Indian trade policy as previously, India's trade barriers mostly took the form of quantitative restrictions. After 1991, the Government of India further reduced trade barriers by lowering tariffs on imports. In the post-liberalization era, quantitative restrictions have not been significant.

Causes

a) The trade deficit in 1991 was US $9.44 billion
b) The current account deficit was US $9.7 billion
c) The gulf war led to much higher imports due to rise in oil prices.
d) Cost pull inflation
e) Political and economical instability

Steps taken by government

a) Established a dual exchange regime

In March 1992 the government decided to establish a dual exchange rate regime and abolish the EXIM scrip system. Under this regime, the government allowed importers to pay for some imports with foreign exchange valued at free market rates and other imports could be purchased with foreign exchange purchased at a government mandated rate.

b) Followed a floating exchange rate system .

In March 1993 the government then unified the exchange rate and allowed, for the first time ,the rupee to float. From 1993 onward, India has followed a managed floating exchange rate system. Under the current managed floating system, the exchange rate is determined ostensibly by market forces , but the RBI plays a significant role in determining the exchange rate by selecting a target rate and buying and selling foreign currency in order to meet the target.

The 2011 Devaluation

The point is that will 2011 devaluation will be considered a major devaluation in the history of India with a much deeper impact.

It was rupees 43.96 against a dollar in the July end and at for $1 is rupees 54.3

Causes

a) Withdrawal of FII's

Foreign Institutional Investors withdrawal from domestic economy is the one big reason for this depreciation.

b) Strengthening of dollars

The Euro-Zone crisis has weakened the Euro significantly against the US Dollar. In other words Dollar is getting stronger in the world markets. Obviously the investors are considering US as safe place to invest in.

c) Other capital flows:

On month by month basis, FDI, ECB's and Foreign Currency Convertible Bonds recorded a slowdown in financial year 2011.

d) Indian Politics:

Number of Indian scams distracted government's concentration away from economy. All these scams make the bad image of India in the global market.

Policy option with RBI to control devaluation of rupee:

a) Raising Policy rates:

The rationale was to prevent sudden capital outflows and prevent meltdown of the currencies. In India's case, this cannot be done as RBI has already tightened policy rates significantly since Mar-10 to tame inflationary expectations. Higher interest rates along with domestic and global factors have pushed growth levels much lower than expectations. In its Dec-11 monetary policy review, RBI mentioned that future monetary policy actions are likely to reverse the cycle responding to the risks to growth. India's interest rates are already higher than most countries anyways but this has not led to higher capital inflows. On the other hand, lower policy rates in future could lead to further capital outflows.

b) Using FOREX Reserves:

RBI can sell forex reserves and buy Indian Rupees leading to demand for rupee. Based on weekly forex reserves data , RBI seems to be selling forex reserves selectively to support Rupee. Its intervention has been limited as liquidity in money markets has remained tight in recent months and further intervention only tightens liquidity further.

c) Easing Capital Controls:

Dr Gokarn Deputy Governor of RBI said in his speech capital controls could be eased to allow more capital inflows. He added that "resisting currency depreciation is best done by increasing the supply of foreign currency by expanding market participation.

Steps taken by Government

a) Increased the FII limit on investment in government and corporate debt instruments.

b) First, it raised the ceilings on interest rates payable on non-resident deposits. This was later deregulated allowing banks to determine their own deposit rates.

c) The all-in-cost ceiling for External Commercial Borrowings was enhanced to allow more ECB borrowings

Administrative measures:

Apart from easing capital controls, administrative measures have been taken to curb market speculation.

a) Earlier, entities that borrow abroad were liberally allowed to retain those funds overseas. They are now required to bring the proportion of those funds to be used for domestic expenditure into the country immediately.

b) Earlier people could rebook forward contracts after cancellation. This facility has been withdrawn which will ensure only hedgers book forward contracts and volatility is curbed .

c) Net Overnight Open Position Limit (NOOPL) of forex dealers has been reduced across the board and revised limits in respect of individual banks are being advised to the forex dealers separately.

Implications of Devaluation:

a) It helps to boost exports

b) It will lead to higher cost of imported goods and make some of the capital extensive projects more expensive to execute

c) It will increase cost of dollar loans taken by companies and increase foreign debt

d) It will slow down the overall economic growth by increasing the interest rates and dissuade flow of FII's

Needs for Devaluation:

Overvaluation of currency associated with import substitution for industrialization as opposed to the export promotion policies.

- The risk of losing competitiveness.
- To relieve on unfavorable balance of trade.
- Economic stabilization.

- Correcting the price distortions.
- To increase competitiveness in foreign markets.
- To raise national income per capita.
- Achieve higher standards of living for their population.
- Close the development gap.
- Government policies of high tarrif on imports fails.
- Cycle of competitive devaluations.

Impact on Indian Economy

This kind of movement leads to high inflation, as India imports around 70% of its crude oil requirement and the government will have to pay more for it in rupee terms. Due to the control on oil prices, the government may not easily pass the increased prices to the consumers. Further, this higher import bill will lead to increase in fiscal deficit for the Govt and will push the inflation, which is already hovering around double-digit mark, which is not good for ordinary people as well. On the other hand, Indian corporate will also have to pay more in rupee terms for procuring their raw materials, despite drop in global commodity prices, only because of a depreciating rupee against dollar.

There are many costs and benefits attached to a stronger and a weaker currency. However, while deciding on a policy, the economic and political situation must also be factored in. In light of the current depreciation of the rupee, one must assign a weightage to the various costs and benefits and then decide whether the depreciation is desirable or not. It is most likely that there will be large support for both views.

Advantages of Rupee Depreciation:

Beneficial to the Exporters

India is majorly involved in exports of handicrafts, gems, jewelry, textiles, readymade garments, industrial machinery, leather products, chemicals and related products. India has been the world's largest processor of diamonds. The exports make a major contribution in foreign receipts.

The companies that are export driven may benefit in terms of better prices for their products and services and be able to increase their profit margins.

For example: if the companies were exporting goods at \$1= Rs 48 they would receive Rs 4800 for every \$100. Whereas, now they would receive

Rs 5135 at current rupee price for every dollar i.e. \$1= Rs 51.35

Moreover the products of Indian exporters would be more competitive in the foreign market and will have an edge over other Asian countries.

Therefore, rupee depreciation should boost the exports.

Good News for NRIs

The fall of Indian rupee is benefiting the NRIs remitting money to India. The salaried workforce abroad can send in more money to their loved ones and their families in India at the same dollar amount.

Currently the Indian rupee is at a 32 month low of Rs. 51.35 against the US dollar in comparison to Rs. 44.1 per dollar during August 2011.

For example: An NRI who remitted \$2000 to his family, in august was able to send Rs 88,000. Whereas, considering the current rupee depreciation he can send Rs 1, 02,700 for the same amount of dollars.

Thus NRIs can enjoy huge benefits from this current rupee fall.

Benefits to the IT Sector

The IT sector being a major job creator in the Indian economy may actually benefit from depreciating rupee as it spells good news for the IT sector. For Information Technology companies, services are billed mainly in dollars or in other foreign currencies. Majorly the companies that hedge funds for a short duration are more likely to benefit from the depreciating rupee.

Hedging of funds means to allocate certain amount of funds as investments in certain securities that are generally speculative in order to earn higher returns Thus, the companies with short duration hedge funds would benefit. Any depreciation of the rupee would peg up their realizations and increase their profit margins.

Benefits to Investors invested in International Funds

The impact of currency movements on an international fund depends on the type of fund and its underlying holdings. These funds will be impacted by the movement of individual currencies, trading and the stock prices, rather than the rupee's behavior against the dollar alone.

However the investors who have invested in funds that have done well despite the market downturn, such as global commodities and gold are more likely to be more beneficial. Like- Birla Sun Life Commodities Equities-Global Precious Metals is up 4.8 percent.

Benefits to the Hotel Industry

Indian Hotels is a dominant player in the luxury and premium business travel space having presence across tier-1 and tier-2 cities, as well as 16 hotels outside the country. It is expected to do well on account of higher room demand, and high average room rates and occupancy rates.

Moreover, with a depreciated rupee an increase in tourists from abroad can be expected as they would have to pay less in rupee terms for their dollars, thus resulting in an increased demand in the hospitality sector.

Disadvantages to Indian Economy

Inflation graph and Fiscal deficit to scale up:

India is suffering from a nearing two digit inflationary pressure. A depreciation rupee will add fuel to this. It leads to high inflation, as India imports around 70 percent of its crude oil requirement and the government will have to pay more for it in rupee terms. Due to the control on oil prices, the government may not easily pass the increased prices to the consumers. Further, this higher import bill will lead to rise in fiscal deficit for the government and will push the inflation.

"It (rupee fall) will be definitely blunt the high base impact. We will have to rework the (inflation) numbers, as we had not taken this into account. We had expected December inflation at 8.2%, but now it could be 8.5% because of the rupee fall," said Abheek Barua, chief economist at HDFC Bank.

Going by a Yes Bank report, every 10% fall in the rupee is likely to lift the inflation rate based on the wholesale price index (WPI) by 40 basis points. Since November 1, the rupee has declined 5.5% against the greenback.

"The rupee has depreciated by about 11% against the dollar during 2011-12 so far. India's imports account for about 22% of GDP and depreciation of the rupee raises the risk of imported inflation," the RBI had said in the October report.

Rupee depreciation has already started to push up prices in some sectors like automobile, consumer goods, and mobile phones. For instance, makers of consumer durables have raised product prices by up to 10%, as their import costs have gone up because of the rupee's depreciation. In the last few months, FMCG firms, including Hindustan Unilever, Dabur, GCPL and Emami have increased prices of their various products by 3 to 10 %. As a result, Indian FMCG firms are turning to efficient cost management and local procurement of raw materials to offset increasing pressure on margins due to the weakening of rupee that has spiked input costs.

A depreciating rupee makes imports of component, capital goods and raw materials more expensive. As inputs and other equipment that are imported get costlier, margins get reduced to that extent. Companies with a high import component and those with foreign currency borrowings may be marked down in the stock market as the rupee depreciates.

The worst affected will be the oil and gas companies and capital goods companies which are net importers. For these companies raw material is in $ terms and sales are in Rupee terms. So, depreciating rupee will have a very adverse impact as this will cause an increase in the cost of raw materials without any corresponding increase in the price of finished products.

A blow to Indian Importers:

India import industry will also have to pay more in rupee terms for procuring their raw materials, despite drop in global commodity prices, only because of a depreciating rupee against dollar. Corporate India is a net borrower of dollar and to that extent a depreciating rupee impacts its balance sheet adversely. Companies with foreign debt on their books are badly impacted. With the rupee depreciating against the dollar, these companies will need more rupees to repay their loans in dollar. This will increase their debt burden and lower their profits. Obviously, investors would do better to stay away from companies with high foreign debt.

Negative impact on FII flows to Indian market:

Rupee depreciation is a huge risk for FIIs who are planning to invest in India. If an FII invest $10000, it can buy stock worth Rs 500000 @ current market price. Consider a scenario where after 1 year, the stock of FII made no loss, no profit and rupee depreciated to 55 against dollar. On stock sale the FII would get Rs 500000, but while converting to dollars, it ends up in loss.

Negative impact on Indian students and travellers abroad:

Individually, travelling abroad becomes more expensive as travel cost can go up by around 10 percent compared to last July figures.

Students studying abroad too will be hit as more rupees will go out to pay for the courses, stay and other

Research Methodology:

To conduct the present survey exploratory research design is used for highlighting the relationship of different variables like FII`s, Forex reserves and GDP on the value of INR. The research enumerates role of Rupee value in the current economic scenario.

Objectives of Study:

- To understand the trend of devaluation of Indian rupee
- To understand the concept of devaluation
- To understand the causes and the steps taken by government on major devaluation that took place in India.
- For highlighting the relationship of different variables like FII's, Forex reserves and GDP on the value of INR.
- To study the impact of devaluation of rupee on the Indian economy

Data Collection Method:

To accomplish the study secondary methods for data collection are used. The Published reports, books, internet websites are used to collect data.

Data Analysis Tool Used:

In the research paper data presented with the help of bar diagrams, charts , graphs and Spearsman Rank correlation method is used to find the relationship between different variables like FII`s, Forex reserves and GDP

Formula Used:

$R= 1- 6\sum D^2/N^3-N$

Limitations of Study:

Less time for study.

Less knowledge of making the research paper.

Trend of Devaluation of INR:

Table No. 3.1

S. No	Year	Value of INR/ 1 $ (yearly average)	Percentage Change
1	2006	45.19	Base year
2	2007	39.42	-12.76
3	2008	48.88	23.99
4	2009	46.47	-4.93
5	2010	46.21	-0.56
6	2011	55.15	19.34
7	2012	57.60	4.44
8	2013 Sept,9	65.25	20.83

Source:RBI

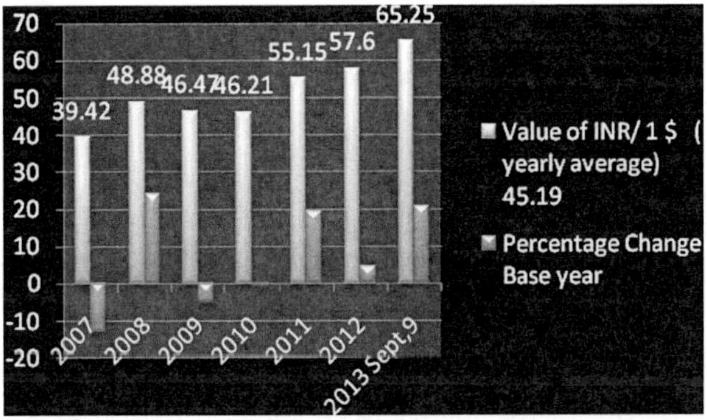

Fig.3.1

S. No	Year	Forex Reserves US (Bn $)	Value of Rs.
1	2008	309.7	48.88
2	2009	252	46.47

S. No	Year	Forex Reserves US (Bn $)	Value of Rs.
3	2010	279.1	46.21
4	2011	304.8	55.15
5	2012	294.8	57.60
6	2013 upto sept	294.5	65.25

The data in table no. 3.1 shows the trend of INR and percentage change during the years in the value of INR. The year 2oo7 shows negative change of 12.76. The value of Rupee during 2007 appreciate to remarkable height due to excessive pressure on the US $ in period of early recession. Then in 2009 it again appreciate due to pressure on the US $. But currently in year 2013 the value of INR depreciate to percentage change of 20.83 against 1 US $. Which exerts the pressure on Indian economy?

Forex Reserves and their Relation to The Value of INR:

Table No. 3.2

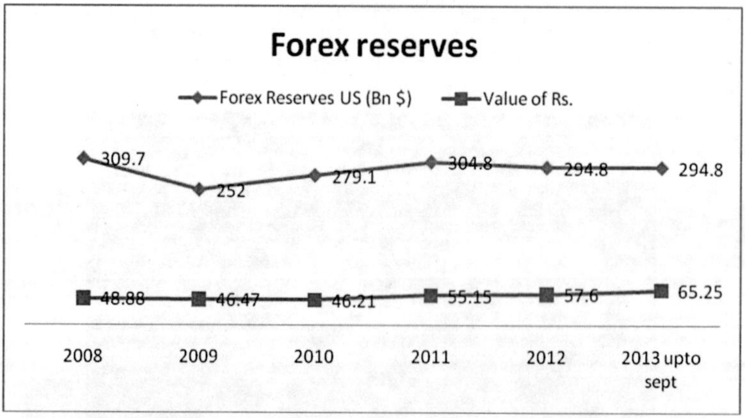

Application of Spearmans Rank correlation method:

r = +0.372

The application of formulae reveals positive relation between the forex reserves and value of rupee. Having direct relation between two i.e if the forex reserves increases the value of rupee appreciate.

GDPs and INR

Table No. 3.3

S. No	Year	GDP	Value of Rs.
1	2008	9.3	48.88
2	2009	6.7	46.47
3	2010	8.4	46.21
4	2011	8.2	55.15
5	2012	6.5	57.60
6	2013 upto sept	5*	65.25

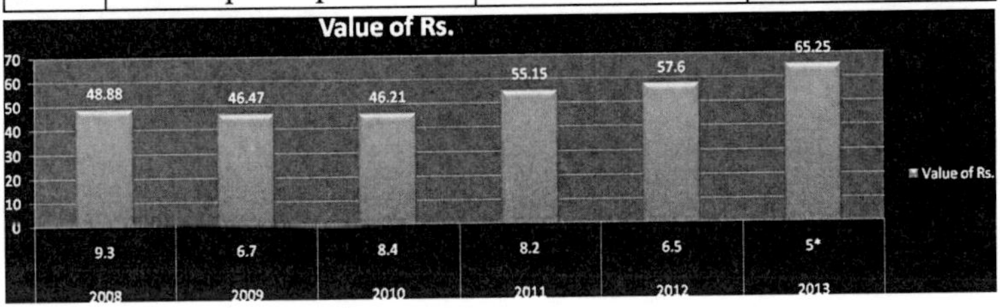

Application of Spearmans Rank correlation method:

r = -0.71

there is high degree of negative correlation between GDP and value of rupee.

FII's& INR:Table No.3.4

S. No	Year	FII's (INR crores)	Value of Rs.
1	2008	66179	48.88
2	2009	-45811	46.47
3	2010	142658	46.21
4	2011	146438	55.15
5	2012	93726	57.60
6	2013 upto sept	168367	65.25

Application of Spearmans Rank correlation method:

r = +0.94

there is high degree of Positive correlation between GDP and value of rupee.

Concusion:

Rupee has to play important role in the destiny of Indian economy. Spurting prices of crude oil in the international market, increasing import of gold and poor economic reforms affects the value of rupee in the international market.Devaluation of rupee is a good sign for exporters , for NRI`s for IT sector and Hotel Industry. While posses certain challenges to Importers, students who want to study abroad, abroad travelers.

Research concluded that devaluation of rupee is also affected by FII's, GDP and Forex reserves. There is a positive correlation between FII`s and Indian rupee, between Forex and Indian rupee whereas there is a negative correlation between GDP and value of Indian rupee. i.e. whenever the investment in FII`s increases the value of rupee appreciates. Similar in case of our Forex reserves whenever there is an increase in Forex reserves value of the rupee appreciates, whereas in case of GDP when the GDP increases the value of Indian currency depreciates.

So Indian government has to take steps to interact FII`s, promoting export activities in the economy and strong structural framework.

References:

- AggarwalAnmol. "Rupee Depreciation: Probable Causes and Outlook." STCI Primary
- Swati Bhatt (2011). Big dangers from a declining rupee." The NEW York time"
- Johri Devika, Miller mark. "Devaluation of the Rupee: Tale of Two Years, 1966 and 1991." State, Market & Economy 84-90

Websites:

www.zenithresearch.org.in

www.sebi.gov.in
www.rbi.org.in
www.wikipedia.org
www.currentaffairsindia.co.in

Social Impact of Globlisation in Developing Countries

Ritu Mankotia

Lecturer of Economics & Management, Department of Applied Science, HIET, Shahpur

Abstract: The period between 1945-1989 was marked by Cold war system and three worlds emerged, namely; first world (US and allies like Western Europe, Canada, Australia, New Zealand and later Japan), second world composed of communist states of Eastern Europe and the Soviet and then the third world which are still occupied with the process of development (O'Briens and Williams 2004, p. 115). However after 1989 to present there are noticeable changes and developments taking place and most scholars have named the 1990s as a decade of globalization. O'Briens and Williams (ibid) argue that, economically new parts of the world have opened to capitalist activities. The spread of capitalist activities has been part of globalization process which ties up well with the liberals believe in the possibility of progress (Baylis, J., et al. (2008, p. 110). The authors provide four components in liberalism theory, namely, juridical, equality, democracy and the free market (p. 116). These are the same values embraced by globalization process to a larger extend. In this paper shows the effects of globalization through the use of Cultural Theory. The aim is to understand its effects on relatonships with especial reference to the developing world – with all the risks of over generalisation this involves.

Keyword:-Social Impact of globalization in developing countries and India

Introduction

The term globalization means International Integration. Globalization is the buzzword in the contemporary world. Broadly speaking, the term 'globalization' means integration of economies and societies through cross country flows of information, ideas, technologies, goods, services, capital, finance and people. Cross border integration can have several dimensions – cultural, social, political and economic. In fact, cultural and social integration even more than economic integration. The focus of this paper is to study the impact of globalization on economic, social and cultural fabric of India.

Definition and methodology

Globalization is a multidimensional phenomenon that not only touches political, economic, social and cultural spheres of any society but also reshapes the traditional way of studying the "social world and human nature" (Robinson, 2005). Globalization is often associated with "intensification of the worldwide social relations", global economic integration, de-territorialization and time-space compression (McGrew, 2008). To measure its extensity and impact on a particular society it is needed to analyze each of these aspects separately.

Economic Impact of globalization in India

Multinational Corporations:

Due to globalization food items are being exported to India in the form of increased consumption of meat, western fast food, sodas and cool drinks, which may result in public health crisis as speculated by certain researchers. The rich biodiversity of India has yielded many healthy foods prepared from locally available organisms. But the marketing by MNCs with large advertisement campaigns lead the people to resort to their products (Mascarenhas, 2003).

- New multilateral agreements for services ,Intellectual properties, communications, and more binding on national governments than any previous agreements. Market economic policies spreading around the world, with greater privatization and liberalization than in earlier decades. Growing global markets in services. People can now execute trade services globally -- from medical advice to software writing to data processing, that could never really be traded before.

Beneficial Effects

Some economists have a positive outlook regarding the net effects of globalization on economic growth. These effects have been analyzed over the years by several studies attempting to measure the impact of globalization on various nations' economies using variables such as trade, capital flows and their openness, GDP per capita, foreign direct investment (FDI) and more. These studies examined the effects of several components of globalization on growth using time series cross sectional data on trade, FDI and portfolio investment. Although they provide an analysis of individual components of globalization on economic growth, some of the results are inconclusive or even contradictory. However, overall, the findings of those studies seem to be supportive of the economists' positive position, instead of the one held by the public and non-economist view.

Trade among nations via the use of comparative advantage promotes growth, which is attributed to a strong correlation between the openness to trade flows and the affect on economic growth and economic performance. Additionally there is a strong positive relation between capital flows and their impact on economic growth.

Foreign Direct Investment's impact on economic growth has had a positive growth effect in wealthy countries and an increase in trade and FDI, resulting in higher growth rates. Empirical research examining the effects of several components of globalization on growth, using time series and cross sectional data on trade, FDI and portfolio investment, found that a country tends to have a lower degree of globalization if it generates higher revenues from trade taxes. Further evidence indicates that there is a positive growth-effect in countries that are sufficiently rich, as are most of the developed nations.

The World Bank reports that integration with global capital markets can lead to disastrous effects, without sound domestic financial systems in place. Furthermore, globalized countries have lower increases in government outlays and taxes, and lower levels of corruption in their governments.

One of the potential benefits of globalization is to provide opportunities for reducing macroeconomic volatility on output and consumption via diversification of risk.

Harmful Effects

Non-economists and the wide public expect the costs associated with globalization to outweigh the benefits, especially in the short-run. Less wealthy countries from those among the industrialized nations may not have the same highly-accentuated beneficial effect from globalization as more wealthy countries, measured by GDP per capita etc. Although free trade increases opportunities for international trade, it also increases the risk of failure for smaller companies that cannot compete globally. Additionally, free trade may drive up production and labor costs, including higher wages for more skilled workforce.

Domestic industries in some countries may be endangered due to comparative or absolute advantage of other countries in specific industries. Another possible danger and harmful effect is the overuse and abuse of natural resources to meet new higher demands in the production of goods.

Technological & Cultural impact of globalization in India.

1. Access to television grew from 20% of the urban population (1991) to 90% of the urban population (2009). Even in the

rural areas satellite television has a grown up market.

2. In the cities Internet facility is everywhere .Extension of internet facilities even to rural areas.
3. Global food chain /restaurants has already found a huge market in the urban areas of India.
4. Lavish Multiplex movie halls, big shopping malls and high rise residentials are seen in every cities.

Technological & Cultural impact of globalization in India.

1. Access to television grew from 20% of the urban population (1991) to 90% of the urban population (2009). Even in the rural areas satellite television has a grown up market.
2. In the cities Internet facility is everywhere. Extension of internet facilities even to rural areas.
3. Global food chain /restaurants has already found a huge market in the urban areas of India.
4. Lavish Multiplex movie halls, big shopping malls and high rise residential are seen in every cities.
5. Telecommunication and Software Industries are booming in India.
6. Entertainment sector in India has a worldwide market. Bellwood movies are distributed and accepted worldwide. Big international companies (Walt Disney,20th Century Fox, Columbia Pictures) are investing on this sector.
7. Famous International brands (Armani, Gucci, Nike, Omega etc.) \are investing in the Indian market with the changing of fashion statement of Indians.

Impact of globalization on agriculture in India

Globalization does not have any positive impact on agriculture. On the contrary, it has few detrimental effects as government is always willing to import food grains, sugar etc whenever there is a price increase of these commodities. Government never thinks to pay more to farmers so that they produce more food grains but resorts to imports. On the other hand, subsidies are declining so cost of production is increasing. Even farms producing fertilizers have to suffer due to imports. There are also threats like introduction of GM crops, herbicide resistant crops etc.

1. 60% of population still depends on agriculture for their livelihood.
2. Occupied 43% of India's geographical areas.
3. Agriculture Scientists are applying new technologies and instruments in growing crops.
4. Different state governments of India are taking initiative to literate the farmers.

Globalisation and Poverty:

Globalisation in the form of increased integration though trade and investment is an important reason why much progress has been made in reducing poverty and global inequality over recent decades. But it is not the only reason for this often unrecognised progress, good national polices , sound institutions and domestic political stability also matter.

Despite this progress, poverty remains one of the most serious international challenges we face up to 1.2 billion of the developing world 4.8 billion people still live in extreme poverty.

But the proportion of the world population living in poverty has been steadily declining and since 1980 the absolute number of poor people has stopped rising and appears to have fallen in recent years despite strong population growth in poor countries. If the proportion living in poverty had not fallen since 1987 alone a further 215 million people would be living in extreme poverty today.

India has to concentrate on five important areas or things to follow to achieve this goal. The areas like technological entrepreneurship, new business openings for small and medium enterprises, importance of quality management, new prospects in rural areas and privatisation of financial institutions. The manufacturing of technology and management of technology are two different significant areas in the country. There will be new prospects in rural India.

The growth of Indian economy very much depends upon rural participation in the global race. After implementing the new economic policy the role of villages got its own significance because of its unique outlook and branding methods. For example food processing and packaging are the one of the area where new entrepreneurs can enter into a big way. It may be organised in a collective way with the help of co-operatives to meet the global demand.

1 Some section of people in India,basically poor and very poor, tribal groups,they did not feel the heat of globalization at all. They remain poor & poorest as they were.
2 Increased gap between rich and poor fuels potential terrorist reaction.
3 Ethical responsibility of business has been diminished.
4 Youth group of India leaving their studies very early and joining Call centres to earn easy money thereby losing their social life after getting habituated with monotonous work.
5 High growth but problem of unemployment. Multi party rule, hence political ideology intervenes globalization (reservation, labor law reforms).
6 Price hike of every daily usable commodities.

Employment Impact

The influx of foreign companies into developing countries increases employment in many sectors, especially for skilled workers. However, improvements in technology come with the new businesses and that technology spreads to domestic companies. Automation in the manufacturing and agricultural sectors lessens the need for unskilled labor and unemployment rises in those sectors. If there is no infrastructure to help the unemployed train for the globalized economy, social services in the country may become strained trying to care for the new underclass.

Impact of Globalization on Indian Culture

Indian culture which in effect means Hindu culture, Hindu religion, Hindu society, Hindu civilization, Hindu way of life are under the lethal threat of the ruthless forces of Globalization today. What went by the name of Colonialism in classical history textbooks produced in the days of British Raj has been replaced today by the synonym of Globalization. The unbridled expansion of western culture has continued at an accelerated rate along with the denigration and decline of Hindu culture, civilization, religion, art, literature and customs. This new Colonialism has taken on several new faces or rather put on new masks. It cleverly masquerades itself through labels and slogans like democracy, humanitarian rights, gender equality, internationalism, free trade and humanitarianism. In the name of modernization and Globalization it pretends to be uplifting peoples whom it is really exploiting. This is not very different in either kind or intent from old Western Colonialism ‘ British Imperialism in the Indian context ‘ which vaunted itself as the benign bringer of Civilization and culture to the uncivilized world. It was given the glorious title of 'White Man's Burden'.

Where does Indian stand in terms of Global Integration?

India clearly lags in globalisation. Number of countries have a clear lead among them China, large part of east and far east Asia and eastern Europe. Lets look at a few indicators how much we lag.

1. Over the past decade FDI flows into India have averaged around 0.5% of GDP against 5% for China 5.5% for Brazil. Whereas FDI inflows into China now exceeds US $ 50 billion annually. It is only US $ 4billion in the case of India
2. Consider global trade - India's share of world merchandise exports increased from .05% to .07% over the pat 20 years. Over the same period China's share has tripled to almost 4%.

3. India's share of global trade is similar to that of the Philippines an economy 6 times smaller according to IMF estimates. India under trades by 70-80% given its size, proximity to markets and labour cost advantages.
4. It is interesting to note the remark made last year by Mr. Bimal Jalan, Governor of RBI. Despite all the talk, we are now where ever close being globalised in terms of any commonly used indicator of globalisation. In fact we are one of the least globalised among the major countries - however we look at it.
5. As Amartya Sen and many other have pointed out that India, as a geographical, politico-cultural entity has been interacting with the outside world throughout history and still continues to do so. It has to adapt, assimilate and contribute. This goes without saying even as we move into what is called a globalised world which is distinguished from previous eras from by faster travel and communication, greater trade linkages, denting of political and economic sovereignty and greater acceptance of democracy as a way of life.

Impact of Globalisation on Indian Business Culture

The Indian economy had been booming for the past few years. The country held great promise for the future. Liberalized foreign policies had unleashed the entrepreneurial spirit of its people and many multi-national firms, attracted by the dusty plains of Deccan, had already set up big offices throughout the nation.

The foreign culture can have both positive and negative influence on people and business firms. New ways of thinking and working may develop leading to higher efficiency. A few examples of impact of foreign culture on business practices are given below:

- Indian companies adopting international accounting standards.

- Just-in-time and other more efficient techniques of inventory control.
- Flexitime and new practices of human resource management.
- Social responsibility and business ethics ideas.
- Improvement in corporate governance practices.
- Customer relationship management practices.
- Inflow of foreign funds.
- Healthy competition with foreign products.

The business sector in India is highly promising in the present scenario. The impact of globalization has changed the business procedure in India in terms of psychology, methodology, technology, mindset work culture etc. Newer challenges, newer opportunities are day-by-day in front of Indian industries, which are profitable and prospective.

The fundamental scope of doing business in India is lying with its people. The huge population of India has created a large unsaturated market of consumers. This is one of the reasons why global companies are very much interested in doing business in India. In the post globalization era this scope has increased immensely for global multinational companies as Government of India has also played a very crucial and supportive role in this respect through liberalized policies and legislative structure.

Let us glance through a few situations that have arisen in India post liberalization

1. Shifting of Agriculture worker to industry sector
2. Urbanization –People are shifting from rural to urban areas.
3. Opening up of trade market –export import boom.
4. Big open saturated market for products
5. A growing market for high quality and low price product
6. Gradual increase of organized retail chain.
7. Growing number of Merger and Acquisitions.
8. Lucid license policies for overseas Multinational Corporation.
9. High growth rate is showing economic prosperity in India.

10. Indian Market leaders going global.

But there are certain negative impacts occurred aftermath the globalization impact in India, which are as follows –

1. Unequal distribution of wealth disparity in income.
2. Rapid privatization government driven public sector units are on sale.
3. Uneven growth in respect of different sectors.
4. Extreme mechanization is reducing demand for manual labours.
5. Both employee and consumer exploitation are on rise by private sector.

The Merits of Globalization are as follows:

There is an International market for companies and for consumers there is a wider range of products to choose from.

Increase in flow of investments from developed countries to developing countries, which can be used for economic reconstruction.

Greater and faster flow of information (through TV, Internet) between countries and greater cultural interaction has helped to overcome cultural barriers.

Technological development has resulted in reverse brain drain in developing countries.

India gained highly from the LPG model as its GDP increased to 9.7% in 2007-2008. In respect of market capitalization, India ranks fourth in the world.

The Demerits of Globalization are as follows:

The outsourcing of jobs to developing countries has resulted in loss of jobs in developed countries as a result, now they are following protectionism measures, for example USA is stopping BPO. There is a greater threat of spread of communicable diseases.

There is an underlying threat of multinational corporations with immense power ruling the globe. For smaller developing nations at the receiving end, it could indirectly lead to a subtle form of colonization.

Even after globalization, condition of agriculture has not improved. The share of agriculture in the GDP is only 18%. The number of landless families has increased and farmers are still committing suicide.

Global recession impact on Indian economy resulted in loss of jobs in IT Sector.

Swami Vivekananda, who foresaw the hazards of globalization and impact of MNC culture in India as early as in 1893 when he spoke at the Parliament of World Religions in Chicago. Here are the golden verses for you,"'Shall India die? Then, from the world all spirituality will be extinct, all sweet-souled sympathy for religion will be extinct, all ideality will be extinct ; and in its place will reign the duality of lust and luxury as the male and female deities, with money as its priest, fraud, force, and competition its ceremonies, and human soul its sacrifice. Such a thing can never be'. Precisely such a terrible thing is taking place in India today on account of the inexorable and immutable process of Globalization".

Conclusion

1. Flowing with globalization ,India is shining in nearly every perspects.
2. India is getting a global recognition and slowly moving towards to become a major economic and political strength.
3. Though the development is progressing rapidly,still many basic problems like rural poverty,corruption and political instability remained unsolved.

Overwhelming impact of globalization can be observed on the Indian culture? Every educated Indian seems to believe that nothing in Hindu India, past or present, is to be approved unless recognized and recommended by an appropriate authority in the West. There is an all-pervading presence of a positive, if not worshipful, attitude towards everything in western society and culture, past as well as present in the name of progress, reason and science. Nothing from the West is to be rejected unless it has first been weighed and found wanting by a Western evaluation. "Swami Vivekananda foresaw the dangers of Globalization as early as in 1893 when he spoke at the Parliament of World Religions in Chicago. To quote his soul-stirring words: 'Shall India die? Then, from the world all spirituality will be extinct, all sweet-souled sympathy for religion will be extinct, all ideality will be extinct; and in its place will reign the duality of lust and luxury as the male and female deities, with money as its priest, fraud, force, and competition its ceremonies, and human soul its sacrifice. Such a thing can never be'." Precisely such a terrible thing is taking place in India today on account of the inexorable and immutable process of Globalization. In the end we can say that, every step of movement towards economic, political and cultural modernization, taken by the state in India, is responded to by the people with an enhanced sense of self-consciousness and awareness of identity. Cultural modernization, sponsored by the forces of globalization, is resented if it encroaches upon or does not promote the core cultural values of society, its language, social practices and styles of life. The vigour of the renewed sense of self-awareness generated among the members of the local cultures and communities is such as to succeed in making adaptive reconciliation with the forces of globalization. The linkages both visible and invisible, defining the cultural interdependence among communities and regions in India which have existed historically, reinforce instead of threatening the national identity. These bonds seem to become stronger as India encounters the forces of modernization and globalization.

References

1. Article on "Theorizing Globalisation" by Douglas Kellner – web source: http://www.gseis.ucla.edu/faculty/kellner/papers/theoryglob.htm

2. Wikipeida The free Encyclopedia- web source: http://en.wikipedia.org./Westernization
3. Article on "Brave New MC World" by Carla Binion – web source: http://www.peace.ca/bravenewmcworld:htm
4. Doing Business in India: A cultural perspective – web source: httm://stylusinc.com/business/India/business_india.htm
5. Herald Tribune – the world's daily newspaper – Globalisation brings new cultural traits to India, by Thomas Fuller - web source:
6. Bhargava P and Dave A, Inequalities in Rural Development: study of Rajathan, Southern Economist, February 1, 2003, P5.
7. Buggi C, Reddy S and Gowda G, Impact of Globalization on Agrarian class structure. Its implications of Indian villages. Third Concept, January 2001, P 17-19.
8. Deaton A. Is World Poverty falling? Southern Economist, January 2003, P. 21.
9. Mascarenhas M. Unpalatable truth. The Hindu, June 22, 2003 p.1.
10. Mohammed C and Nazar M, The Role of Multinational corporations, Southern Economist, February 1, 2003. P.24

Abramovitz, M. (1986), "Catching-up, Forging Ahead and Falling Behind", Journal of Economic History, vol.46, pp.385-406.

Economics Reforms and its impact on Software Industry

Vivek Chaudhary

Faculty of Computer Science, Govt. College Dharamshala

viveksalil@gmail.com

Sandeep Kumar

Faculty of Computer Science, Govt. College Dharamshala

Ssrana369@yahoo.co.in

Abstract: The economics reforms, introduced in India by then Finance minister Dr. Manmohan Singh laid the foundation for growth of software sector in India. The reforms help the Software Industry to grow at rapid pace. After the reforms companies used the concept of Software technology park of India (STPI). Many Bureaucrats hurdles were removed. The reforms resulted in availability of financing from the equity root. After economic reforms, companies were allowed to decide IPO prices using market driven price earning ratio. Another important change was the introduction of current account convertibility.

The RBI eased restriction on accessibility of foreign currency. This made it easier to hire foreign consultants and establish sale offices abroad. The number of overseas offices of Indian Information technology Companies increased rapidly. Multinational companies were allowed 100% ownership of subsidiaries in India.

Different software giants such as Oracle, SAP, Microsoft, Sun and IBM established their centers in India. It results in intense competition for talent. Indian software companies adopted world class quality processes, tools and methodologies. Duties and tariffs were reduced and tax structure simplified. Import structure was simplified and most items were brought under open general license.

This paper discusses in detail all the areas of economic reforms and its impact on software industry.

Keywords: Software, Economic reforms, Software technology park of India, Information Technology

India Before Economic reforms:

Before 1991, India adopted an inward looking policy. The policy makers were confused regarding the intentions of private sector. Further imports were restricted. At one point of time , the marginal tax rate was as high as 97% , wealth tax was as high as 8% and estate tax was 85%. In addition the corporate sector faced numerous bureaucratic hurdles. There were number of factors which are not in favor of Private sectors. Information Technology sector faced difficulties in accessing even basic infrastructure such as phones or data communication lines.

Economic reforms of 1991:

The economic reforms in India refers to ongoing economic reforms in India that started on 24 July 1991. After Independence in 1947, India adhered to socialist policies. Attempts were made to liberalize the economy in 1966 and 1985. The first attempt was reversed in 1967. Thereafter, a stronger version of socialism was adopted. The second major attempt was in 1985 by Prime Minister Rajiv Gandhi. The process came to a halt in 1987, though 1967 style reversal did not take place. In 1991, after India faced a balance of payments crisis, it had to pledge 20 tonnes of gold to Union Bank of Switzerland and 47 tonnes to Bank of England as part of a bailout deal with the International Monetary Fund (IMF). In addition, the IMF required India to undertake a series of structural economic reforms. As a result of this requirement, the government of P. V. Narasimha Rao and his finance minister Manmohan Singh (currently the Prime Minister of India) started breakthrough reforms, although they did not implement many of the reforms the IMF wanted. The new neo-liberal policies included opening for international trade and investment, deregulation, initiation of privatization, tax reforms, and inflation-controlling measures

The fruits of liberalization reached their peak in 2007, when India recorded its highest GDP growth rate of 9%. With this, India became the second fastest growing major economy in the world, next only to China. The growth rate has slowed significantly in the first half of 2012. An Organization for Economic Co-operation and Development (OECD) report states that the average growth rate 7.5% will double the average income in a decade, and more reforms would speed up the pace.

The economic reforms introduced in 1991 laid the foundation for the growth of software sector in the country. The reforms abolished many restrictive boundaries for business. It decentralized power to regional and state offices. Further it encouraged better industry orientation among bureaucrats. The reforms resulted in availability of financing from the equity route. For the first time, companies were allowed to decide IPO prices, using market driven , price earning ratios. RBI also eased restrictions on accessibility to foreign currency. It made it easier to hire foreign consultants.

The IT Sector:

IT refers to digital processing storage and communication of information of all kinds. For all these processes software is required. Therefore software and IT can be used in every sector of economy. IT and software has major impact on economy not only in developed countries but also in developing countries such as India. In India Software exports has grown dramatically despite the country 's relatively overall low level of income and development. The software used in different IT enabled services such as different kind of data processing , voice interactions remote sensing banking and so on. From 2008 till now the revenues of IT and software industry has grown rapidly. In year 2012 aggregate IT software and services revenues is estimated at USD 88 billion.

Within the global software industry, India was able to increase its market share from 51% in 2009 to 58% in 2012. Information technology is playing an important role in India today & has transformed India's image from a slow moving bureaucratic economy to a land of innovative entrepreneurs.

The IT sector in India is generating 2.5 million direct employment. India is now one of the biggest IT capitals of the modern world and all the major players in the world IT sector are present in the country.

The year 2012 is Milestone year for Indian IT-BPO industry- aggregate revenues cross the USD 100 billion mark, exports at USD 69 billion.

- Export revenues (including Hardware) reached USD 69.1 billion in FY2012 growing by over 16 per cent; Domestic revenues (including Hardware) at about USD 31.7 billion, growing by over 9 per cent.
- Software and services revenues (excluding Hardware), comprising nearly 87 per cent of the total industry revenues, generated USD 87.6 billion in FY2012; estimated growth of about 14.9 per cent over FY2011.
- Within Software and services exports, IT services accounts for 58 per cent, BPO is nearly 23 per cent and ER&D and Software Products account for 19 per cent.
- The industry continues to be a net employment generator – added nearly 230,000 jobs in FY2012, thus providing direct employment to about 2.8 million, and indirectly employing 8.9 million people.
- As a proportion of national GDP, the sector revenues have grown from 1.2 per cent in FY1998 to an estimated 7.5 per cent in FY2012.

- The industry's share of total Indian exports (merchandise plus services) increased from less than 4 per cent in FY1998 to about 25 per cent in FY2012.
- While the global macroeconomic scenario remained uncertain, the industry exhibited resilience and adaptability in continually reinventing itself to retain its appeal to clients.

Software Industry:

i) Domestic Revenues:

The basic distinction in IT is between hardware and software. The former refers to physical components such as processors, storage devices and communication devices. The latter refers to the instructions that govern the flow and processing of information. The design of hardware actually involves the development and use of appropriate software. India's software industry services largely enhanced by the economic reforms of 1991. Much of the software demand came from abroad however the software industry‘s domestic revenue also grew rapidly. The National Association of software and services Companies (NASSCOM) project domestic sales over 50% of industry sales and it is the impact of recent growth in domestic software. Much of this growth was driven by demand from sate Governments, which are introducing e-governance initiatives. The second largest sector is financial sector.

India's IT firms -- Infosys, Wipro, Tata Consultancy Services (TCS) -- propelled Indian industry and the economy into global view. It expanded faster than any other industry through the decade, growing from $150 million in 1991 to more than $5.7 billion in 2000. The rapid growth, the new technologies adopted and the expansion in both competitors and value-chain partners made it an exhilarating time. In just a few years, we built the IT and operational infrastructure that had taken US companies decades to put in place, and by the late 1990s we were competing in operational excellence and scale not just with each other, but also with Western firms. The early predictions for Indian IT were rosy—the home-grown IT sector was expected to lead to technology and knowledge spillovers across the economy, and trigger a widespread trend in electronification and IT-led surges in productivity. But in the early 1990s, our growth, though dramatic, was also quite isolated. There were continued restrictions on capital and labour that limited the ability of India's industries to invest in technology. Diffusion rates of such technology as a result stayed low, with the vast majority of Indian companies spending less than 1 per cent of their turnover on IT.

ii) Software exports:

India's software exports went from a few million dollars in 1980's to over a billion dollar by 1995-96 and over 69 billion dollar in 2012. India's software export capabilities include the depth of its base and breadth of its global reach. There are over 2000 Indian software exporters. The TCS, Infosys, Wipro, Satyam and HCL) are approaching the status of global brands. While US remains the largest market for Indian software exports , its share of software exports is 62% with Europe at 24% and Japan and rest of world accounting for the remaining 14%. Individual firms and organizations such as NASSCOM are targeting new markets such as Germany.

iii) Strengths of Indian Software Industry:

- One of the largest pool of technically qualified high class IT manpower
- Enormous skilled human resource compared to developed countries leading to lower manpower cost nearly one tenth of those in developed nations, thus giving India a comparative advantage.
- Offers a wide range of services from support / data processing to sophisticated software systems etc.
- Rich experience of working with large global companies and enjoy high credibility

- Expertise on a wide variety of platforms
- Accommodating nature of Indian IT workforce.

Impact on India's growth:

IT sector has become one of the most significant growth catalysts for the Indian economy. In addition to fuelling India's economy, this industry is also positively influencing the lives of its people through an active direct and indirect contribution to the various socio-economic parameters such as employment, standard of living and diversity among others. The industry has played a significant role in transforming India's image from a slow moving bureaucratic economy to a land of innovative entrepreneurs and a global player in providing world class technology solutions and business services. The industry has helped India transform from a rural and agriculture-based economy to a knowledge based economy.

Key Highlights

- Fast emerging as a growth story driven by a growing middle class, consumer spending, and technology innovation
- Increasing adoption of technology and Telecom by consumers and focused Government initiatives – leading to increased ICT adoption.

The numerous examples of successful pilot e-governance programs and their impact on Indian economy include the following:

- Computer aided registration of land deeds and stamp duties in various states reducing reliance on brokers and possibilities of corruption.
- Computerization of rural government offices.
- Computerized checkpoints for local entry taxes with data automatically sent to a central database .
- Consolidated bill payments sites allowing citizen to pay bills from electricity to university bills.

- E-mail requests for repairs to basic rural infrastructure.

References:

1) NASSCOM "The software Industry in India"
2) NASSCOM " The Software industry in India, Strategic review"
3) Economic survey of India-Ministry of finance ,Government of India.
4) http://www.nasscom.org
5) http://www.tcs.com/news/tcs-media
6) Dey,Ataru.2000"New telecom policy"
7) Dossani,Rafiq and Martin Kenny "Creating an environment :Developing venture capital in India"
8) Kumar,Nagesh 2000 "New technology based small service enterprises and employment: The case of Software and related services Industry in India".
9) Rao,M.Govinda and Nirvikar Singh 2000 "How to think about local Government reforms in India:Incentives and Institutions".
10) P Bardhan - OUP Catalogue, 1999 - ideas.repec.org
11) J Bhagwati - OUP Catalogue, 1993 - ideas.repec.org
12) K Basu - 2004 - books.google.com
13) C Chakraborty, P Nunnenkamp - World development, 2008 – Elsevier
14) Afxentiou, P C and A Serletis. (1991), 'Exports and GNP Causality in the Industrial Countries: 1950-1985', Kyklos, 44, 2, pp. 167-79.
15) Ahluwalia, Montek S. (2002): "Economic Reforms in India since 1991: Has Gradualism Worked?", Journal of Economic Perspectives, Vol. 16, No 7, pp. 67-88.
16) Alston, Richard M.; J. R. Kearl, and Michael B. Vaughan. (1992): "Is There a Consensus Among Economists in the 1990's?" Amer. Econ. Rev. (Papers and Proceedings), 82:2, pp. 158-77.
17) Anwer, M S and R K Sampath. (2001), 'Exports and Economic Growth', Indian Economic Journal, 47, 3, pp. 79-88.

The Present Paper is An Attempt E-Banking

Vipan Kumar Bhulal

Asst. Professor Govt.pg College, Hamirpur

Abstract: E-Banking is rapidly expanding its wings across the globe and India is no exception to this phenomenon. Now, several banks have put their electronic banking facilities on the Internet and are providing many facilities like funds transfer between accounts , Billing payments, Web-shopping, Railway and air-ticket booking, etc to their customers at the click of a button. But since Web is a public space open to all.

So, Internet Banking is the need of the hour and private banks are already providing efficient Internet Banking Services to their customers. Although Public sector banks are also providing Internet Banking Services but the number of their branches facilitating such services are less as compared to private banks. So, the Public sector banks should concentrate more on providing Internet Banking services. By taking the above measures Internet Banking will become more secure and will help the banks to become more competitive and profitable.

The present paper is attempt to study the access the present scenario of the services of Internet Banking, scope of Internet Banking in future, problems faced by the consumers in availing the Internet Banking Services and to access the satisfaction level experienced by the users of Internet Banking Services.

Introduction

Earlier people would be tired standing in along queue waiting for a passbook to be updated or they would wait for the next day for the demand draft to be prepared but now Internet Technology has invaded the portals of our banking institutions and as the cliché goes everything will just be a click away. No doubt, innovations like telebanking and automated teller machines (ATM's) have considerably put customers at ease on the recent past. But with net banking the customer will be able to transact with the help of a mouse and his visits to the neighbourhood bank will become a thing of the past.

In the age of electronic technology the regular application of computing, wireless communication, networking, etc, in the banking field has brought revolutionary change in the traditional ways banks do business. Today, your bank can serve you at home, or allow you to serve yourself from anywhere. You can draw your money from ATM's, you can check your accounts through the Internet, and you can phone the bank to send you a representative. Not only that, your physical bank which is still around-suddenly seems to be doing a lot more things than just banking. It is technology that is making all this possible. Internet banking has gained wide acceptance internationally and seems to be fast catching up in India with more and more banks entering the fray. This is why, most, most modern banks instead of merely dealing with financial deposits and loan apply promote, and distribute the want-satisfying products, services and ideas to start its journey towards development of computer and other technology based digital economy since 1960 to ensure quality service to its customers.

Technology –The Governing Factor

It is the technology that is making easy operation of banks. Even 10 years back, banks would have found it impossible to provide even basic banking services to millions of small and medium customers with all their branches. At the back end technology is freeing bank employees to concentrate on value-added work rather than just mundane necessities. Today, technology offers options where banks can almost literally address a market of one with a customized product or service. Though a modest start has been made in India, net banking has still a long way to go. This development has been acknowledged by the latest Online Banking Report, which features a listing for ICICI Bank .Some others have also endeavored to make real time banking a reality before this century closes.

Reasons why new private and multi-national banks have been able to survive, thrive, and adapt in an increasingly competitive space.

These banks were able to leverage on low-cost channels such as ATM's and Net Banking to the optimum levels contributing to reduced operating costs. The cost of transactions over channels like ATM's and the Internet are lower than doing it through the branches-Banks have realized that shifting customer access to lower cost channels can help bring down operating costs. These channels are used not only to improve customer service but also to divert traffic from the branches.

Customers using ATM's, phones and the Internet not only allow banking transactions, but also cross-selling of other financial products and services. For example, if the cost of a branch banking transaction is taken at Rs 100/-, the cost of an ATM transaction would be around Rs 30/-, phone banking around Rs 20/-, and internet banking around Rs 5/-.But this does not mean that branch banking is obsolete. Rather, banks are reinventing their business models to offer new financial services through its branches.

At the back-end, technology is freeing bank employees to concentrate on value-added work rather than just mundane necessities. In computerized banks, once a transaction is posted it is auto-reconciled. This system is easy and frees people to concentrate on other customer services.

New Horizons

The important factor that is causing a shift in the industry is that of conveniences for the consumer. People need timely access to banking services, and have less time to spend at banks, and prefer the convenience of long distance banking. Of course, society's view of what is convenient is changing .People were accustomed to associating convenience with doing business in their neighbourhood, and not traveling to a bank across town. Now, however, society has a different definition of bank convenience. Also, we should mention it is directly due to mergers that banks are able to offer more full service branches, and ATM machines. This is more convenient to the customers, and creates bank loyalty.

Increased use in ATM's , the growing use of home and office computers, fax machines, and point of sale terminals allowing consumers to make transaction electronically is now considered convenient. Thus, branch location is no longer a priority from the consumer's view.

Objective of The Study

1. To access the present scenario of the services of Internet Banking.
2. To study the scope of Internet Banking in future.
3. To study the problems faced by the consumers in availing the Internet Banking Services.
4. To access the satisfaction level experienced by the users of Internet Banking Services.

Research Methodology

Purpose of the study: the main purpose of the study is to analyse the preferences of people regarding e-banking services.

Sample Design: The sample design for my study is Descriptive

Sample Unit: Individuals who are availing Internet Banking Services. (Hamirpur)

Sample Size: 70 respondents

Sampling Method: Non-Probabilistic convenience sampling.

Sources of Data: The data was collected from both primary and secondary sources.

Primary Data: The primary data collection was done through the survey method. The survey was conducted using the questionnaire method.

Secondary Data: Secondary data was collected from the following sources:

a) Books on Internet Banking
b) Internet
c) Journals

Data Analysis tool – I have analyzed the data by using Pie charts & Bar Charts

Limitation of Study

1. Time constraints was the main limitation of the study.
2. Sample size is not significant as it is very small.
3. As in this study convenient sampling is used which shows business.
4. Sample unit is confined to only one particular area.

Data Analysis and Interpretation

Table-I

No. of users who have availed the ATM facility of any Bank

Availed The Facility	No. of Users
YES	90%
NO	10%

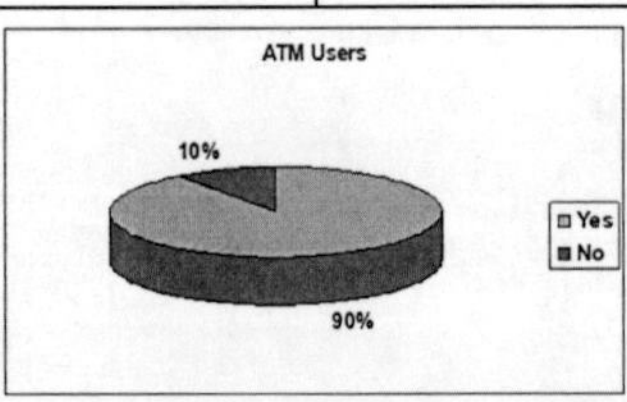

Interpretation

- 90% users are availing the ATM Services.
- 10% users did not avail the ATM Services.

TABLE-II

The users have used the ATM facility of the following banks:

Name of The Bank	No. of Users in Percentage
Hdfc Bank	25
State Bank of Patiala	25
Icici Bank	10
Bank Of Punjab	15
State Bank Of India	15
Not Used The Facility of ATM of Any Bank	10

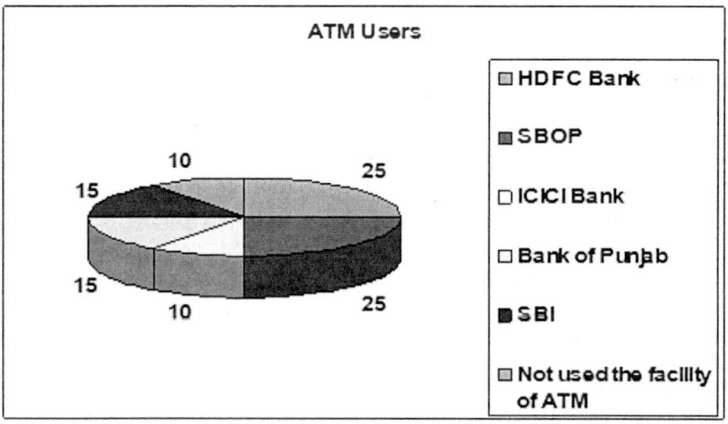

Interpretation

- 25% users avail the ATM services of HDFC Bank.
- 25% users avail the ATM services of State Bank of Patiala.
- 15% users avail the ATM services of Bank of Punjab.

- 15% users avail the ATM services of State Bank of India.
- 10% users did not avail the ATM services of any bank.

Table-III

The satisfaction level experienced by the ATM users

Level of Satisfaction	No. of Users in Percentage
Highly Satisfied	20
Satisfied	70
Indifferent	0
Dissatisfied	0
Highly Dissatisfied	0
Users Not Availing The Facility	10

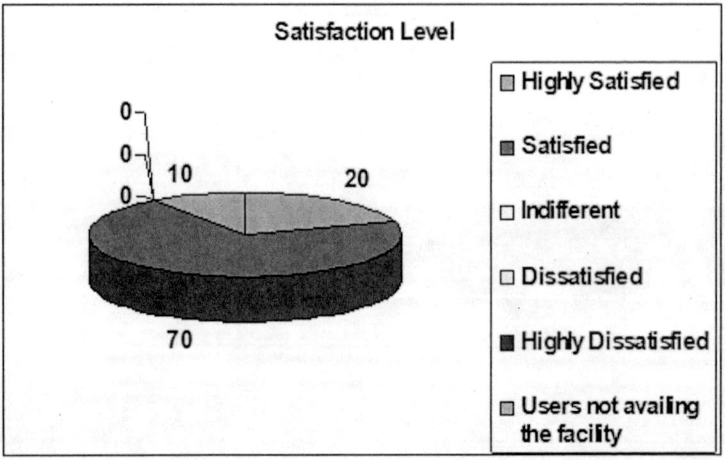

Interpretation

- 20% users are highly satisfied with the ATM Services.
- 70% users are satisfied with the ATM Services.
- 10% users did avail the ATM Services.

TABLE-IV

Following number of times in a week the users have used the ATM:

Number of Times	Number of Users in Percentage
1	60
2	20
3	5
5	5
Users not availing the facility of ATM	10

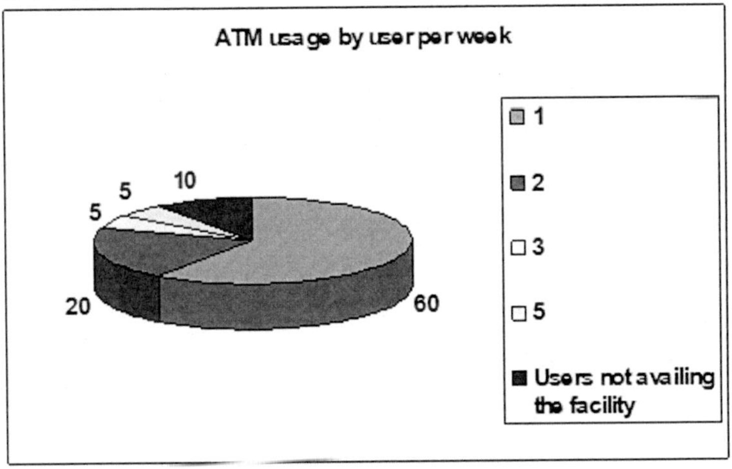

Interpretation

- 60% users avail the ATM Services within 1 week.
- 20% users avail the ATM Services within 2 weeks.
- 5% users avail the ATM Services within 3 weeks.
- 5% users avail the ATM Services within 5 weeks.
- 10% users did not avail the ATM Services.

TABLE-V

Preference of the users of ATM card of the benefits of ATM:

Benefits of ATM	Number of Users in Percentage
It is time-saving	20
It is beneficial when cash is needed Urgently	60
It is convenient	20

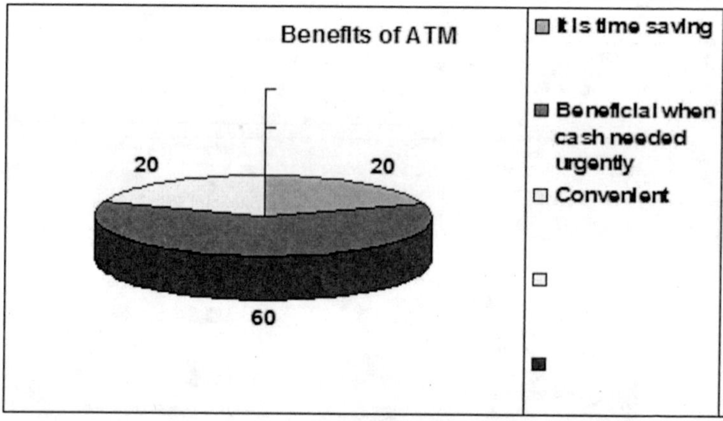

Interpretation

- 20% users believes that ATM Services are time saving.
- 60% users believed that it is beneficial when cash is needed urgently.
- 20% users believed that it is convenient in nature.

TABLE-VI

Whether the users of ATM card have faced any problem while using the ATM card:

YES	40% (No. of users)
NO	60% (No. of users)

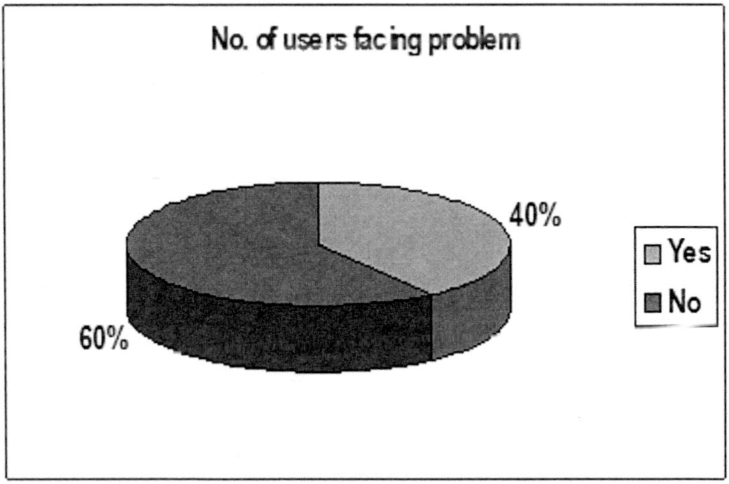

Interpretation

- 40% users faced the problems while using ATM Services.
- 60% users faced the problems while using ATM Services.

Problems faced by the users:

Nature of Problem	No. of users in Percentage
The card got withheld in the machine	25
ATM was not working	63
Instructions to use the ATM were not clear and received no help from employees of the bank	12

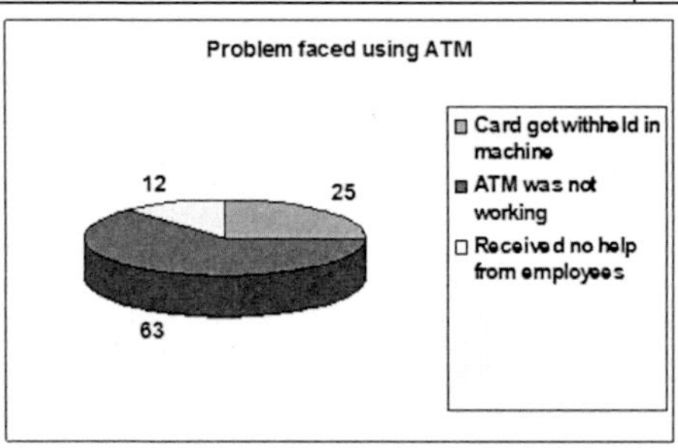

Table-VII

Other Internet Banking Services availed by the respondents:

Nature of Service	No. of Users in Percentage
Credit card	15
Transferring one's money from one city to any other branch in a city	5
Opening Fixed Deposit account via the Internet	10
Inquire about the balance in one's saving, Current and FD account	0
Tax deducted at source on one's FD account for current financial year	0
Giving instructions over the internet for stopping payments on cheques	0
Request for a cheque book via the internet	5
View all transactions on an account for a specified period and get a copy via e-mail	0
None of the above	65

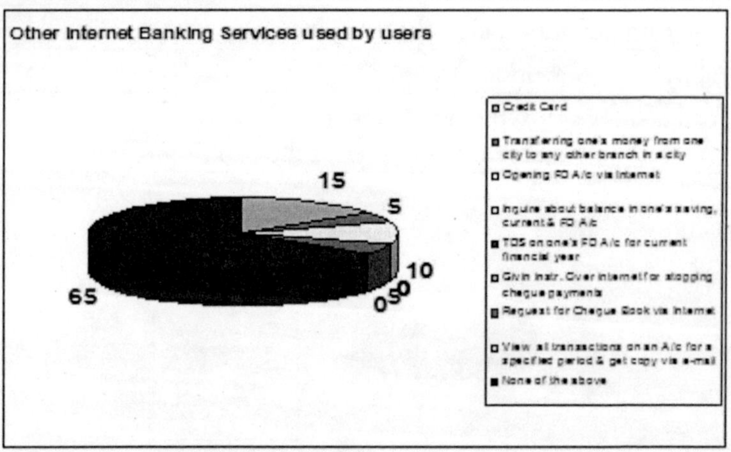

Interpretation

- 15% users avail the credit card facilities.
- 5% users transfers the money from one branch of the city to another branch of the other city.
- 10% users open their FD accounts through Internet.
- 5% users request for cheque books through Internet.
- 65% users did not avail for any other E-Banking Services.

Table-VIII

Whether the respondents ever had any grievance against the bank providing Internet Banking Services to it:

Yes	5% (No. of Users)
No	95% (No. of Users)

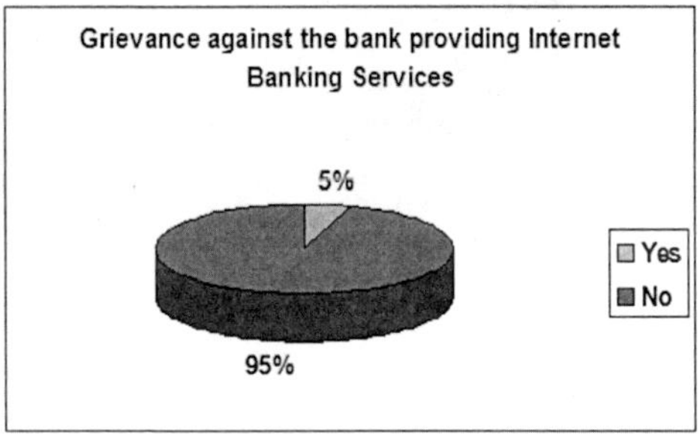

Interpretation

- 5% users have grievance against the banks providing E-Banking Services.
- 95% users have not grievance against the banks providing E-Banking Services

Table-IX

Level of satisfaction experienced by the respondents of the grievance handling procedure of the bank:

Level of Satisfaction	No. of Users in Percentage
Highly Satisfied	0

Level of Satisfaction	No. of Users in Percentage
Satisfied	100
Indifferent	0
Dissatisfied	0
Highly Dissatisfied	0

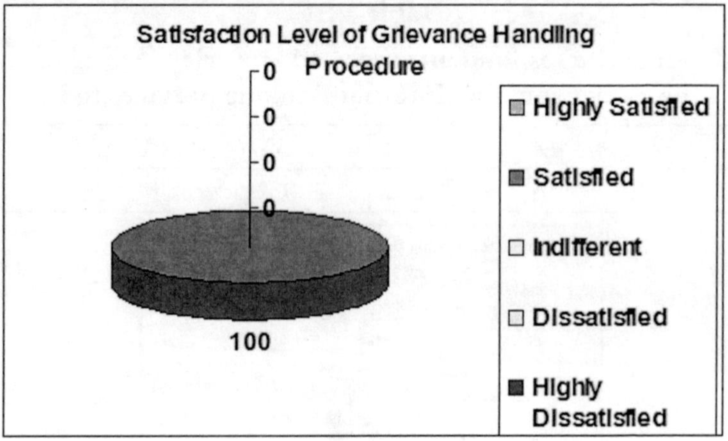

Interpretation

- 100% users are satisfied with the level of grievance handling procedures of banks.

Table-X

Respondent's opinion of the weaknesses of Internet Banking Services:

Nature of Weakness	No. of Users in Percentage
There is only one way communication	44
The security is not flawless	30
Lack of first hand experience gained by a person by visiting a bank is not there	26

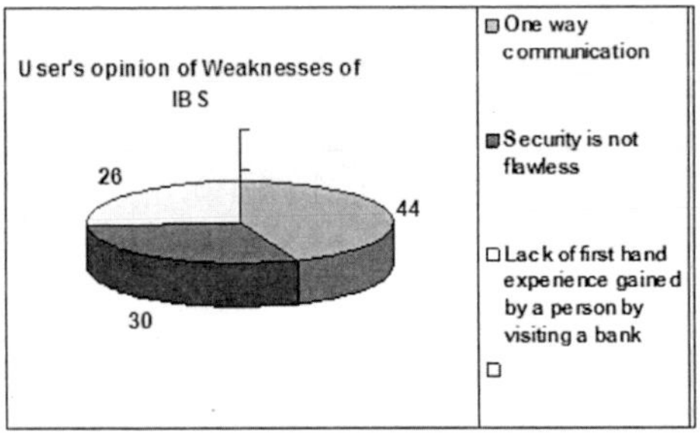

Interpretation

- 44% users believes that there is one way communication in E-Banking.
- 30% users believe that security is not flawless in E-Banking.
- 26% believes that there is lack of first hand experience gained by visiting banks.

Table-XI

Respondent's view of the security of the Internet Banking Services:

It is secure	45% (No. of respondents)
It is not secure	55% (No. of respondents)

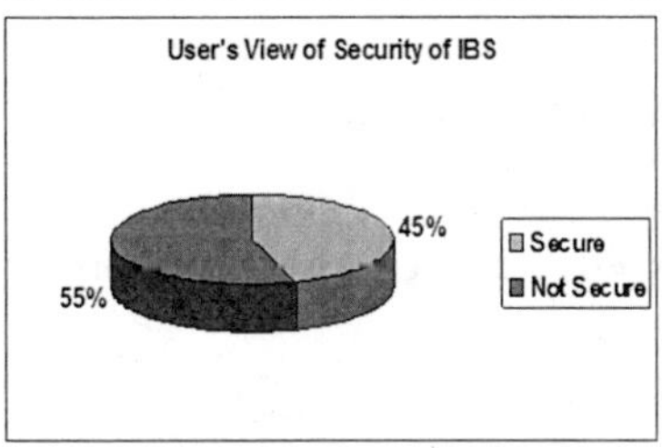

Interpretation

- 45% users believe that E-Banking Services are secured.
- 55% users believe that E-Banking Services are not secured.

It is secure because

The security systems are reliable	89% (No. of Respondents)
There are firewalls which strengthens the security system	11% (No. of Respondents)

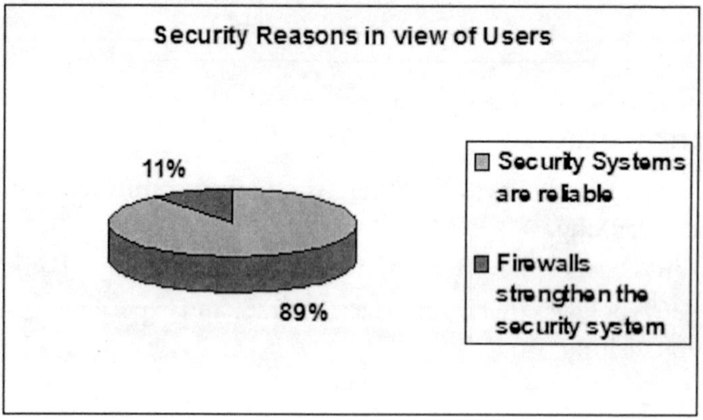

Interpretation

- It is secured because 85% users believe that security systems are reliable.
- It is secured because 11% users believe that firewalls strengthen the security system.

1 Respondents who are of the opinion that the internet banking is not secure.

Table-XII

Opinion of the respondent's on whether all public sector banks should start providing Internet Banking Services to survive in the market:

Answer of The Respondents	No. of Users in Percentage
Yes	75
No	25

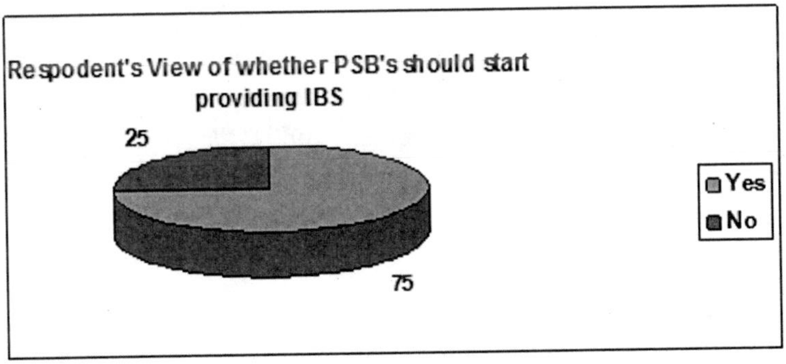

Interpretation

- 75% users are in the opinion that all public sector banks should start providing E-Banking Services.
- 25% users are in the opinion that there is no requirement of E-Banking Services by the public sector banks.

Respondent's reason for saying yes in the above table:

Respondent's Reasons	No. of Users in Percentage
Internet Banking is time-saving	20
To face the competition	50
Internet Banking is convenient and hassle-free	20
Customer preference and increasing of number of people using the internet	10

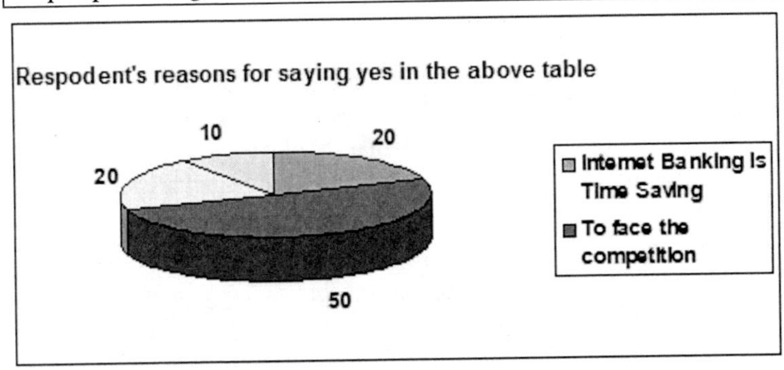

Interpretation

- 20% believe that E-Banking is time saving.
- 50% believe that it is helpful in facing competition.
- 20% believe that it is convenient and hassle free.
- 10% believe that customers prefer using Banking Services through Internet.

Conclusion

E-commerce is rapidly expanding its wings across the globe and India is no exception to this phenomenon. Now, several banks have put their electronic banking facilities on the Internet and are providing many facilities like adopting ECS and EDI for knowing account-status , funds transfer between accounts , Billing payments, Web-shopping, Railway and air-ticket booking, etc to their customers at the click of a button. But since Web is a public space open to all , THESE INTENET BASED SERVICES ALSO RAISE NEW THREATS FOR THE BANKS. Financial institutions like banks and merchant websites like Rediff , Amazon , payment sites like PayPal etc,. by virtue of the value of information , their customers share with them are becoming the most lucrative target for the attackers. Attackers are formulating newer strategies for attack and one such attack is Phishing.

References

Library Sources

1. Internet Banking-The Second Wave: By Sanjeev Singhal,Tata Mcgraw Hill Publication, 2003
2. Management Trends (A Journal of Department of Business Management) Article- Internet Banking by Kavita Kshatriya Sep 2004
3. Indian Banking 2005 , The ICFAI University Press Publication
4. The Journal of Internet Banking and Commerce (Published by Array Development of Ottawa)

5. International Journal of Business Performance Management 2002 (Published by Inder Science publishers)
6. Internet Banking Shopping for the Older Generation by ---- Greg Chapman
7. Internet Banking : Strategies, Tools and Best Practices – by Mona Brewer (Published by Sheshunoff and Co.)

Internet Sources

www.sbi.com

www.hdfcbank.com

www.icicibank.com

www.firstib.com

www.nationalcity.com

www.netbanker.com

Corporate Governance in Cooperative Bank: A Case study of Kangra Central Cooperative Bank H.P.

Dr. Pooja (Assistant professor)

Regional centre Dharmshala (H.P.)

Email:pooja_5702@yahoo.in

Abstract: Corporate Governance refers to the system by which corporations are directed and controlled. Governance is a mechanism for monitoring the actions, policies and decisions of corporations. The word corporate Governance has come up mainly in the wake up of economic reforms characterized by liberalization and deregulation. Corporate Governance has at its backbone a set of transparent relationship between an institution's management, its board, shareholders and stakeholders. Governance provides the structure through which corporations set and pursue their objectives, while reflecting the context of the social, regulatory and market environment. The purpose of this paper is to examine the factors that influence the governance in cooperative banks. Good governance within the organization is a need of the hour. To conduct a study on governance practices in such banks, a leading cooperative bank i.e. Kangra central cooperative bank of HP has been taken. Exploratory research design has been used to satisfy the research objectives. To meet the purpose sample size of 75 employees of IT and establishment (HR) department has been selected from various branches of KCC bank Dharmshala. The study is based on both secondary as well as primary data obtained through personal interview. To analyze and interpret data pie charts and chi square is used. This study has also analyzed the factors behind job satisfaction level of employees and their awareness towards government policies .Further this research helps to find an insight to the Government practices in the cooperatives banking sector. This study would help the government decision makers to work more upon the considered determinants to improve the Governance in the banks.

Introduction

Governance

Good governance term is defined as "the manner in which power is exercised in the management of a country's economic and social resources for development". Sustainable development can only take place if a predictable and transparent framework of rules and institutions exist for the conduct of private and public business.

Good governance ensures that political, social and economic priorities are based on broad consensus in society and that the voices of the poorest and the most vulnerable are heard in decision-making over the allocation of development resources.

Good corporate governance is largely affected by the size of the economy, differences in the legal, regulatory, institutional, financial and political framework, status of the capital market, stakeholder's perception and many more.

Majority of companies have reported that the governance changes had a strong and substantial impact on organization efficiency. If bank managers face sound governance mechanism, they will be more likely to allocate capital efficiently.

The elements of good governance constitute participation, rule of law, transparency, responsiveness, consensus orientation, efficiency, accountability and strategic vision. The element

"Participation" states that all men and women should have a voice in decision-making, freedom of association and speech. "Rule of law" states that legal framework should be feared and enforced impartially particularly the law of human right. "Transparency" states the free flow of information, enough information should be provided to the individual asking for. "Responsiveness" means serving to all stakeholders. Although it has been observed that it is tough to have implementation of all the elements of good governance in an organization.

Major elements of good governance which may influence the organization working

Banks are the dominant industry, important drivers for economic growth, most important sources of finance and main depository for the economy's savings. Corporate and local governance principles and practices are most significant in the banking industries compared to other industries. Few of them are followed

Good board practices: This relates to clearly defined roles and authorities, clearly defined duties and responsibilities of directors, appropriate composition and mix of skills, appropriate board procedure, board self evaluation and training.

Control environment: This covers establishment of independent audit committee, presence of risk management framework, internal control procedures, internal audit function and establishment of management information system.

Transparent disclosure: This refers to disclosure of financial information, disclosure of non-financial information along with web based disclosure.

Board Commitment: This covers creation of corporate governance committee, commitment of appropriate resources, use of policies and procedures.

In simple words corporate governance is the system by which companies are directed and controlled. Adopting corporate governance 's best practices improves access to external financing, lowers the cost of capital, improves operational performance, increases firm valuation, improves share performance and reduces the risk of corporate crisis.

Ensuring Good corporate governance is largely dependent on the legal and regulatory framework, political priority, economic condition and cultural traditions. Conceptually, governance can be defined as the rule of the rulers, typically within a given set of rules. One might conclude that governance is the process by which authority is conferred on rulers, by which they make the rules, and by which those rules are enforced and modified.

In various places, good governance has been associated with the democracy and good civil rights, with transparency, with the rule of law with the efficient public services. Good governance encompasses the role of public authorities in establishing the environment in which economic operators function and in determining the distribution of benefits as well as the relationship between the ruler and the ruled.

Indian Scenario

The corporate governance initiative in India was not triggered by any serious nationwide financial, banking and economic collapse. The initiative in India was driven by The Confederation of Indian Industry. In December 1995, CII set up a task force to design a voluntary code of corporate governance. The final draft of this code was widely circulated in 1997. In April 1998, the code was released. It was called "Desirable Corporate Governance: A Code". Following CII's initiative, the Securities and Exchange Board of India (SEBI) set up a committee under Kumar Mangalam Birla to design a mandatory-cum-recommendatory code for listed companies. The Birla Committee Report submitted in February 2000 and it was approved by SEBI in December 2000. The report became mandatory for listed companies through the listing agreement and implemented according to a rollout plan. Following CII and SEBI, the Department of Company

Affairs (DCA) modified the companies Act 1956, to incorporate specific corporate governance provisions regarding independent directors and audit committee.

Corporate Governance in Banking Sector

The corporate governance practice is important for banks in India because majority of the banks are in public sector, where they are not only competing with one another but with other players in the banking system. Further, with restrictive support available from the government for further capitalization of banks, many banks may have to go for public issues, leading to transformation of ownership. The banks form an integral part of the economy of the country and any failure in a bank might have a direct bearing on the financial health of the country. The Basel committee on banking supervisory authorities was established by the Central Bank Governors of the G10 developed countries in 1975. The Basel committee in the year 1999 had brought out certain important principles on corporate governance for banking organizations which, more or less have been adopted in India. The minimum impact of recession on Indian economy was because of strong and effective nature of banking sector in India.

Indian Co-operative Banks:

An important segment of the organized sector of Indian banking .The segment is represented by a group of societies registered under the Acts of the States relating to co-operative societies. Cooperative banking institutions take deposits and lend money in most parts of the world. The origin of the co-operative banking movement in India can be traced to the close 19th century when, inspired by the success of the experiments related to the cooperative movement in the Britain and the cooperative credit movement in Germany, such societies were set up in India. Co-operative banks are an important constituent of the Indian financial system. Some are the primary financiers of agricultural activities, some small-scale industries and self employed workers. Different types of cooperative credit or non credit societies are operating in India. Further co operative credit societies are classified into A)Rural credit societies which are primarily agricultural; B)Urban credit societies which are primarily non agricultural. For the purpose of agricultural credit there are different co-operative credit institutions to meet different kinds of needs. Short & medium term credit is provided through three tier federal structure. At top is the apex body i.e., state cooperative Bank; in the middle there are district co-operative banks or central co-operative banks, at the grass root level i.e., village level there are primary agricultural credit societies. For medium to long term loans to agriculture, specialized co-operative societies have been formed. These are called 'Land Development Bank '

Kangra Central Co-operative Bank:

The Kangra Central Co-operative Bank came into existence on 17 March, 1920. The bank has made a reputation in the domestic markets for its wide services. It is one of the oldest bank in Himachal Pradesh working in Kangra , Hamirpur, Una,Lahoul Spiti and Mandi districts. The head office of the Kangra Cooperative bank has been situated at the Dharmshala, district Kangra HP. The bank has 166 branches and 14 Zonal offices. In January 1956, Indore banking union was emerged and then the second branch of bank was opened at Nurpur. Thereafter, in January 1957 Palampur banking union was emerged and third branch of bank was opened at the Palampur. In October 1958, Nadaun banking union was merged and fourth branch of bank was opened at Hamirpur. KCC bank is countered among the leading bank in Himachal Pradesh. The brand has toiled hard in the past to prove its metal in the field of customization, by time and again taking the end successfully overcoming challenges that proved rather too much for competing banks. As far as the organizational structure is concerned, they have their head office located at Dharmshala, 14 Zonal offices, 166 branches and 16 extension counters.

Objectives of the study:

Primary objective of the study

To examine various factors that influenced the governance in cooperative banks.

Secondary objectives are:-

To study the awareness level of employees towards governance.

To study the job satisfaction level of employees.

Research design

Research design is planning for research. It is the conceptual structure within which study is conducted. A research design is the arrangement of conditions for collection, interpretation and analyses of data in a manner that aims to combine relevance of research purpose with economy in procedure. This paper examines the satisfaction level of employees and their awareness towards policies ofbank. To accomplish the objectives exploratory research design has been used.

Scope of study

The study is confined to Himachal Pradesh, particularly Dharmshala region

Research Methodology:

Type of data: the source of data collection in the study is primary as well as secondary.

Primary source: The primary data has been collected through interviews and questionnaire of various employees of IT and establishment department. Secondary source: The secondary data has been collected from reports, magazines and hand outs. Apart from the key sources relevant materials have been collected through the internet also.

Sample design:

For this study, convenience sampling has been used. The total sample size is 75. There are 100 employees working in the head office of KCC bank, Dharamshala. But the actual responses we could get 55 and 20 from IT and establishment department respectively. Hence the sample size taken is 75 from KCC, Bank, Dharamshala Kangra HP.

Tools of analysis:

The tools used for the study are pie chart, percentage method and chi square test to measure the goodness of fit.

Data Analysis and Interpretation

Here an effort has been made to examine the factors that influence the governance in Kangra Cooperative Bank.

Satisfaction level of employees

There are many ways to inspire the employees and increase their satisfaction for example employee's orientation, positive work environment, relative competitive benefits, workforce engagement, develop skills, recognition & reward, awareness of new government policies. These all factors are also the part of corporate governance. Following table shows the satisfaction level of employees in Kangra Central Cooperative Bank in regard these factors

Table 1

Satisfaction level of the Employees

Responses / Employees	Yes	No	Total
IT Department	25	30	55
HR Department	8	12	20
	33	42	75

x^2=.77<0.05(3.84)

It is noted that less than half i.e. 44% (33) employees from both department are satisfied whereas majority of the employees i.e. 42 are not satisfied. Further table shows that the calculated value of x^2 is .177 which is less than the table value at 5% level of significance. It means there is no difference in the opinion of employees of IT and HR (establishment) department regarding job satisfaction.

Reasons for non-satisfaction among employees

Various reasons which has been put forth by bank employees for non satisfaction are shown in table 2

Table 2

Reason for non-satisfaction among employees

S. No.	Responses / Employees	Employees	In %age
1	No performance based incentives	25	60%
2	Transfer limited to branch office	09	21%
3	Lagging behind in technology implementation	05	19%
	Total	42	100%

From the table 2 it can be concluded that the main reason behind non satisfaction among employees is no provision of performance based incentives whereas other reasons are transfer limited to branch offices and lagging behind in technology implementation respectively.

Figure 1

Reasons of non-satisfaction among employees

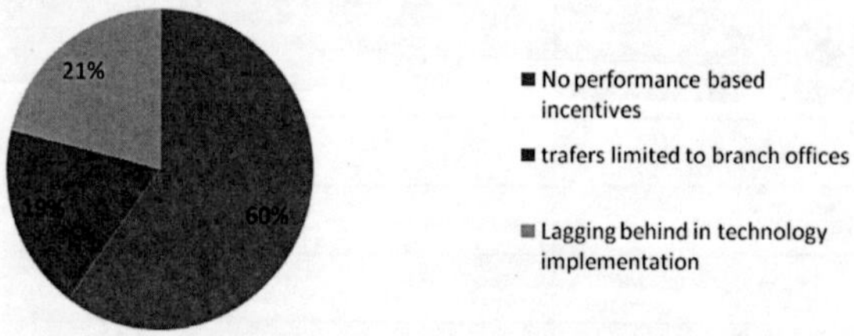

It is evident from the above tables and charts that the employees are not fully satisfied with their jobs but they are certainly aware of the Governance policies. To compete with the other banks, co-operative banks should also introduce the technologies as and when they are launched in other banks. Apart from this, they should introduce performance based incentive schemes.

Late Implementation of Technology

Different opinions of employees regarding late implementation of technology in the bank. Competitive implementation of technology is a sign of good governance. Following table shows the views of KCC Bank employees regarding the implementation of technology whether the bank was late or advance in comparison to other banks in implementation of technology

Table 3

Timely implementation of technology

Responses / Employees	Yes	No	Total
IT Department	31	24	55
HR Department	14	06	20
	45	30	75

$X^2 = 1.136 < 0.05(3.84)$

The table depicts that 60% i.e. 45 KCC Bank employees think that bank was very late in implementation of technology, whereas 40% think that Bank has implemented the technology well in time. Further it is seen that the calculate value of x2 i.e. 1.136 is much less than the table value i.e. 3.84 at 5% level of significance. It means there is no significant difference in the opinion of IT employees and establishment (HR) employees regarding the late implementation of technology.

Views regarding introduction of performance based incentive schemes.

This is one of the major factors in corporate Governance. Higher the performance, higher the incentives. It develops motivation in other employees for higher performance. Following table shows the responses regarding introduction of performance based scheme.

Table 4

Introduction of Performance based incentive schemes

Responses / Employees	Yes	No	Total
IT Department	40	15	55
HR Department	18	02	20
	58	17	75

$X^2 = 2.48 < 0.05(3.84)$

Table shows that 58 i.e. 77% employees are in favour of introduction the performance based incentives in the banks whereas only 17 i.e. 23% employees are not in favor because they all are old employees.

The calculate value of Chi-square is much less than the table value i.e. 3.84 at 5% level of significant difference in the IT and establishment (HR) department employees regarding the provision of performance based incentives. It means the employees of both departments are in favour of introduction of performance based incentives.

Quick Redressal of grievance complaints

How quickly the grievances of employees are handled. This is the part of good governance.

Table5

Quick Redressal of Grievance Complaints

Responses / Employees	Yes	No	Total
IT Department	40	15	55
HR Department	16	04	20
	56	19	75

$X^2 = 0.406 < 3.84$

Here it is seen that majority of the KCC bank employees i.e. 75% admitted that their grievance are handled quickly, whereas only 25% has neutral opinion which is negligible. Further it is seen that the calculated value of x^2 is 0.406, which is much less than the table value 3.84 at 5% level of significance. It means there is no significant difference in the opinion of IT and establishment (HR) department employees regarding the redressal of grievance complaints. It means that employees are fully satisfied with the management in the quick redressal of grievance complaints.

Transparent system of working

This refers to disclosure of financial information, disclosure of non financial information along with web based disclosure

Table 6

Transparent system of working

Responses / Employees	Yes	No	Total
IT Department	45	10	55
HR Department	15	05	20
	60	15	75

$X^2 = 0.43 < 3.84$

Table 6 depicts that vast majority of employees i.e. 80% think that there is a transparent system of working in the KCC Bank.

The calculated value of x^2 is much less than the table value 3.84 at 5% level of significance. It means there is no significant difference in the opinion of IT and establishment (HR) department employees regarding the transparent system of working.

Findings:

The research shows the following results:

- There is no performance based incentive schemes which lowers the moral of employees.
- The implementation of technology is being done late while the other banks have already taken a lead.
- The bank has maintained a transparent system of working which contribute the good governance.
- The management is efficiently handling the grievance complaints.

Conclusion:

This study examined the various factors which can influence the governance in KCC Bank, Dharamshala. Study shows that majority of employees are not satisfied with KCC Bank. Main reason found behind non satisfaction, is no performance based incentives. These are all young employees who want such incentives and they all are right because such incentives are the main source of motivation. The employees who are denying implementing such schemes are old. Second reason is transfer limited to branch office, though fresh employees want job rotation all over Himachal. Last reason they have given that KCC Bank is always lagging behind in technology in comparison to commercial banks. But majority of bank employees admitted that KCC Bank handled quickly the grievances of employees and posses transparent system of working which may be a sign of good governance , still there is no independent grievance cell for effective & quick redressal of grievances. So we conclude that KCC Bank has good governance but not up to the mark.

Bank should make every possible effort to satisfy its employees because young employees are fixed asset of the bank. This paper further helps to find an insight to the governance practices in the co-operative banking sectors.

This study has contained limitations, some of which have been mentioned below:

- Limited sample size: our study is limited only to the Dharamshala region of Himachal Pradesh. Researchers can consider other braches too to know the goodness of governance in various banks.
- Questionnaire has been used and there is no way of telling how much a respondent thought has put in.

Recommendation:

We recommended that the following steps for better governance in co-operative banks

- The bank should establish independent grievance redressal cell with toll free number for effective & quick redressal of grievances by the customers, employees & other stakeholders.
- Performance based incentive schemes should be introduced in co-operative too like Private Banks. This will be helpful in minimizing the defaulters.
- Presently District Co-Operative Banks are governed majority by three bodies namely RBI, NABARD and State Government; single agency/body should govern the bank.
- Among the policies, the collection period of NPA should be reduced to at least one month. According to "Securitization Act 2005", processing time for collecting back assets is around six to seven months. If this processing period is reduced, the NPA can further be reduced.
- Quick implementation of technology, with respect to other banks.
- Unlike Nationalized banks, they don't have any credit cell/ recovery cell. They can think of brining such cells into

co-operative banks too. The reasons being, this factor can reduce NPA to greater extent.

- The time gap should be reduced in providing the basis incentives namely promotions, increments to the employees.
- At present, only in I.T. Department they are considering the specialized people for recruitment. This criterion should be followed in other departments too.

References:

- KCCB official websites http://www.kccb.in
- http://web.worldbank.org/WEBSITE/EXTERNAL/COUNTRIES/MENAEXT/EXTMNAREGTOPGOVERNANCE/0"contentMDK:20513159~pagePK:34004173~piPK;34003707~theSitePK:497024,00.html
- http://web.worldbank.org/external/default/main?theSitePK=497024&region=119229&piPK=64172092&pagePK=64169512&menuPK=497048&topic=644283&sortDesc=DOCDT
- http://documents.worldbank.org/curated/en/210/01/16818818/corporate-governance-success-stories-ifc-advisory-services-middle-east-north-africa

http://en.wikipedia.org/wiki/Cooperative_banking

Factors Influencing Foreign Direct Investment in Indian Tourism Industry

Sandeep Walia

Assistant Professor, (Tourism & Management)

Maharaja Agrasen University, Baddi, Himachal Pradesh

sndp.walia551@gmail.com

Abstract: Foreign Direct Investment (FDI) has taken a centre space in Indian subcontinent. Various industries in India have witnessed inflow of lot of funds through FDI. Keeping in view the relevance of FDI an effort has been made to undertake a study over factors that influence the flow of FDI in Indian tourism industry. The study is based on a survey conducted through a structured questionnaire. The questionnaire included 42 statements, on which the opinion was obtained. The collected data was analyzed with the help of SPSS package. Factor analysis was conducted to arrive at the main factors out of all. The results revealed four key factors that influence FDI in Indian tourism industry. These actors are perception and infrastructure, government and policy, economy, and competitiveness. The results of the study can prove to be very useful for the industry as well as the government to attract more FDI in the tourism industry and help it grow further.

Keywords: Foreign Direct Investment, Tourism, Industry

Introduction

Foreign Direct Investment (FDI) is a feature that is ever-present in tourism industry (Chen and Devereux, 1999). FDI can be defined as when an investor based in one country acquires an asset in another country with the intent to manage the asset (Naudé and Krugell, 2003). FDI remains paramount for developing nations, especially India as it aspires to remain global, as well as to achieve exponential growth in number of tourists.

The South African tourism industry has been valued very high in terms of turnover and is expected to rise sharply as the private sector is also contributing to the investment along with the government. Investment opportunities in Indian tourism industry are found in hotels, guesthouses, resorts, theme parks and game lodges. Ecotourism is also proving to be an excellent opportunity for investment and development. Foreign investors are attracted towards the growth rate of foreign visitors in India showcasing a higher potential for better return on investment. Growth in number of tourist arrival has helped increase value and return on investment. It has also led to India's rising popularity as a tourist destination for its Monuments, Natural beauty, Diversity, Heritage etc.

Indian tourism industry is proving itself to be an ideal tourist destination with many FDI opportunities. The opportunities identified in India are encompassing the value for money, good infrastructure, and a stable economy (FDI Magazine, 2003). The latest initiative to improve India's economic performance is the latest growth policy.

The present research has been conducted with an aim to identify the key factors that influence the inflow of FDI in the Indian tourism industry. These factors identified in the study can assist government agencies to successfully attract and invite more FDI as well as to remain competitive globally. These factors can also assist other researchers who are working in the similar areas to get a better understanding of this aspect of Indian tourism industry.

Investment in the tourism industry is supposed to be highly capital-intensive. It is said to be capital intensive as a lot of investment is required to build up infrastructure and facilities to attract tourists. For example huge capital is required to erect resorts, hotels, motels, restaurants, shopping centre, places of amusement and guesthouses. However an investment in existing tourism offerings rarely appears in the media. According to Snyman (2007) these include offerings such as game farms, holiday homes and wine farms etc. Added to this is the fact that these offerings are used for private as well as business purposes.

It is also relevant to differentiate between the providers of infrastructure for tourism such as the hotel and transport sectors, and the packagers and sellers of tourism products such as tour operators and travel agents. The hotel and transport are such sectors that require heavy initial investment, for example, the building of the hotel and its fittings, the aircrafts for the airlines etc. one will be able to recover investment only over a period of number of years (Vellas and Bécherel, 1995). The chance for the investment to reap losses instead of profits are high in initial years, which makes the prospective investors afraid (Francis, 1993). Factors that can deter potential investors to invest are the following:

1. inadequate government support;
2. a lack of supporting infrastructure;
3. insufficient investment incentives;
4. excessive time required to obtain decisions;
5. a multiplicity of agencies, many with overlapping functions;
6. a lack of adequate local expertise; and
7. difficulties in tackling complex land tenure systems;
8. in adequate training schemes (UNESCAP, 2001).

Increase in inflow of FDI asks for attention to be on the determinants of investment decisions and the related micro and macro economic expectations of the host ecoomy that may be relevant. Researchers such as Eicher and Kang (2005), Saayman and Snyman (2005), Biswas (2002), Cheng and Kwan (2000), Resmini (2000), De Mello (1997), Wang and Swain (1997), UN (1995), Lucas (1993), Veugelers (1991), Petrochilos (1989), Gray

(1987), and Schneider and Frey (1985) have identified some of the micro economic indicators that may influence inflow of FDI in a country these were the micro and macro economic indicators that were identified by the researchers as factors that will influence FDI (Husted and Melvin, 2004; Marx et al. 2003; Bandelj, 2002; Cheng and Kwan, 2000; Resmini, 2000; Urata and Kawai, 2000; Yang et al., 2000; Bhinda et al., 1999; Chaudhuri and Srivastava, 1999; De Mello, 1997; Wang and Swain, 1997; UN, 1995; Amirahmadi and Wu, 1994; Lucas, 1993; Schneider and Frey, 1985).

a) markets size and growth,
b) labour costs,
c) host government policies,
d) tariffs and trade barriers
e) product life cycle.

Macroeconomic indicators such as:

a) openness and exports,
b) exchange rates,
c) inflation rates,
d) budget deficits,
e) investment and infrastructure and
f) political instability

In addition to the above specified macro and micro determinants, factors that influence inflow of FDI in the Indian tourism industry context includes a lot of aspects. These aspects were used to develop a valid questionnaire so as to determine the determinants of FDI inflow in India for tourism industry. It was observed that there is a dearth of research in this area of tourism in India. UNESCAP (2001) researched major aspects related to tourism and economic development along with the development of infrastructure for tourism. Suggested measures for creating a suitable and congenial environment for attracting foreign investment in tourism industry in India were also provided. Heese (2000) investigated trends on investments and offshore investment by the host country. Furthermore, it showed areas of comparative edge as well as a decline in inflow of foreign investment. Additionally, this research also presented the importance of privatisation as a tool for leveraging investment. It also discussed the eminence of mergers and acquisitions.

Researchers Chen and Devereux (1999) used the theoretical model of trade to concentrate on some welfare effects of tourism only for developing economies. The study revealed that tourism could reduce welfare for trade regimes that are dominated by some export taxed or import subsidies, not ignoring the fact that FDI is beneficial especially in tourism industry of India. Research conducted by Kruger-Cloete's (1995) focused on the financing of the development of tourism. Attention was also given to the international experience, which included aspects such as:

a) policy,
b) cultural renaissance,
c) conservation and development,
d) human and environmental sustainability,
e) investment funding and incentives, and
f) the specific requirements of identified areas, for example, infrastructure and land use.

These were studies conducted in the field of FDI in tourism industry. However none of these studies have addressed the key factors that would influence the inflow of FDI in tourism industry.

Research Methodology

The survey was conducted with the help of questionnaires that were filled by different estate agents in Northern India. Only those agents were selected for the study who specialise in dealing with foreign direct investors. Out of all the estate agents 200 agreed to be part of the study and fill the questionnaires, which also eventually became the sample population for this research. All 200 agencies were then contacted obtain their willingness to participate in the research. These estate agencies were sent the questionnaires and out of these 200 agencies 115 agencies actually participated in this survey and had sufficient data on FDIs and responded to the questionnaires positively. The questionnaire consisted of a number of micro and macro aspects that were identified in the preliminary research and a pilot study of (five) questionnaires was conducted to ensure that estate agencies would understand the questions.

The collected data were analysed with the help of SPSS software package. With the help of the software descriptive statistical analyses were performed. The statistical analyses included descriptive analyses and a factor analysis. A principal axis exploratory factor analysis with Promax rotation was performed on 39 statements where four factors were retained, explaining 53.8 per cent of the variance.

Results

The results of the study deal first with a summary of the profiles of the top five countries that invest in India. Thereafter, the determinants of FDI in tourism in India will be presented.

As per the results of the study, it revealed that the primary foreign direct investors are from the UK, Germany, Netherlands, USA and France. It is also interesting to find that majority of tourists that arrive in India are from these countries only. This confirms the research by Mueller (2003) who stated that foreign investors target markets that they have already visited. The results also show that different markets prefer different products even though one notices a common theme. The results reveal that most of these investor nations invest as individuals. It is only a small part of a total investment. An individual investor here means that the investor is the main shareholder (100 per cent) while on the other hand a consortium means here a group of individuals or companies where each has a percentage share in the investment.

Factor Analysis

The factor analysis was conducted on the 42 individual statements and was compressed to four key factors that influence inflow of FDI in India. To determine the appropriateness of principal components analysis (data reduction procedure) for the collected data, a correlation matrix for the motivational data, KMO (Kaiser-Meyer-Olkin) measure of sampling adequacy and the Barlett test of sphericity were also examined. The KMO measure of sampling adequacy aims at examining whether the strength of the relationship between variables is large enough to proceed to a factor analysis. The Barlett test was found to be highly significant ($p<0.00001$). With such high significance data reduction by principal components was found to be legitimate. A factor analysis with promax rotation was thus performed. An eigen value of 1.0 was considered for factor extraction and loadings of 0.30 was used for item inclusion. To check the reliability of the data Cronbach's coefficients was also performed for each factor and to serve as a measure of internal consistency among the items. Cronbach's coefficients above 0.7 indicating reliability (table 1).

Table 1: Cronbach Coefficients of each factor identified

Cronbach's Alpha	0.924	0.823	0.813	0.704

The reason for performing factor analysis is to correlate the statements of the questionnaire and group them together as one factor and study only those factors instead of all. After perfrming the factor analysis four factors were retained. The communalities varied between 0.28 for negotiations and 0.70 for unrest. The factors were then labelled as per the similarity in the elements. Loadings of the factors of climate, scenery, and location were found to be highly significant on more than one factor and were thus removed from the factor analysis. The four factors (Table 2) were labelled as

a) Perception and infrastructure (Factor 1),
b) Government and policy (Factor 2);

c) Economy (Factor 3);

d) Competitiveness (Factor 4);

	FACTORS			
	1	2	3	4
	Perception and infra-structure	Govern-ment and policy	Economy	Competi-tiveness
Level of unrest/distur-bance	0.900			
Crime	0.898			
Political stability	0.686			
Government regula-tions with regard to international buyers	0.686			
Communication infra-structure	0.596			
Foreign exchange	0.594			
Legal rights	0.565			
Availability of Banks	0.551			
INR vs USD	0.476			
Availability of fresh water	0.463			
Location of airports	0.459			
Terrorism	0.459			
Legislation	0.442			
HIV/AIDS	0.375			
Influence of the local situation to sell prop-erties to international buyers	0.368			
Logistics	0.348			
Malaria	0.341			
Improvement of con-stitutional negotiations	0.237			
Business confidence	0.364			

Labour disturbance/ unrest	0.344			
Availability of roads	0.306			
Labour costs		0.618		
Industry charters (BEE)		0.581		
Bureaucracy		0.556		
Level of trained employees		0.552		
Labour laws		0.165		
Market size and growth of the market			0.886	
The state of economy			0.694	
Expected high return			0.634	
Inflation			0.609	
Profitability of the farm/lodge/hotel			0.564	
Interest rate			0.503	
Privatisation/public-private partnerships				0.647
Historical/personal links				0.579
Incentives offered by the government				0.492
Local market size				0.486
Availability of natural resources/raw material				0.473
Entrance to Indian markets				0.452
Growth of international travel to India				0.316

The first factor i.e. Perception and infrastructure, deals with the aspects such as political stability, crime, foreign exchange, communication infrastructure, availability of roads, location of airports and availability of fresh water. Infrastructure as a determinant was also found to be a main motive by researchers such as Cheng and Kwan (2000), UNESCAP (2001) and Urata and Kawai (2000). This factor had the fourth highest mean value (1.96).

The second factor was Government and policy, (with the second highest mean value of 2.61), underlines the notion that this determinant plays a vital role in attracting inflow of FDI. Studies undertaken by Cheng and Kwan (2000), Vickers (2002) and Kruger-Cloete (1995) again support this finding. Government and policy factor includes the country's labour, the new Black Economic Empowerment policy and aspects pertaining to labour cost and training.

Factor 3 was labeled as Economy of the country. It included aspects like inflation, economic outlook, expected returns and market size and growth. Naudé and Krugell (2007) highlighted the fact that a stable economy is a prerequisite for letting the FDI in. This factor had a mean value of 1.94. Mohammed (2006) has also confirmed the latest initiatives to improve the nations's economic performance is seen where tourism is given prime importance.

Factor 4 is labeled as Competitiveness. It is the factor which scored the highest mean value i.e. 2.88. This aspect includes public, private partnerships, incentive schemes, market size, entrance to Indian markets, and growth of international travel. Du Plessis (2002) emphasized on the importance of remaining competitive, especially in the industry that faces severe global competition.

The correlations between the key factors

A correlation matrix was created among the four key factors that were identified after performing the factor analysis. This matrix indicates correlations that have practical significance between factor 1 (Perception and infrastructure) and factors 2, 3, and 4 (Government and policy, Economy and Competitiveness). There is also a significant correlation between Government and policy and Economy, and between Economy and Competitiveness. Economic literature shows that political stability and governance are important factors for FDI (Naudé and Krugell, 2007; Asiedo, 2002). The results are presented in table 3.

Table 3: Correlation matrix of key factors

Factor	(1)	(2)	(3)	(4)
Perception and infrastructure (1)	1.000	0.512**	0.600**	0.419**
Government and policy (2)	0.512**	1.000	0.455**	0.313*
Economy (3)	0.600**	0.455**	1.000	0.455**
Competitiveness (4)	0.419**	0.313*	0.455**	1.000
* significant at 5 % level, ** significant at 10 % level				

Implications and Conclusions

Based on the results of the research conducted, the following implications can be identified. Firstly, a relationship has been identified between travel behavior of tourists and inflow of investment from the home country of those tourists. It therefore seems that once tourists of a country visits a foreign destination, chance of investing increases in the host country. Therefore tourism marketers are also involved in inflow of FDI, but indirectly. Hence empowerment of tourism marketers on the facet of FDI should have a positive impact on increasing investment. Also, tourism information dissemination through brochures, web sites etc. should have information available that is of interest of potential investors. This relationship is, however, an aspect that needs to be further researched. In addition to these implications, this research revealed that climate is also one of the major motivators for investors to invest in India and the same applies to foreign tourists visiting India.

Secondly, even though four main key factors that were identified for use by marketers of FDI, it is pertinent here to highlight that the most important factor out of these four factors is for the tourism industry to remain competitive, followed by complete government backup and support and the need for clear policies and avoiding any ambiguity. These aspects have policy implications in terms of the focus when FDI promotions take place.

Conclusions

The main aim of conducting the present research was to determine the key factors influencing FDI for the Indian tourism industry in order to attract and retain inflow of FDI as well as to be globally competitive. Survey was conducted among the various state agencies that specialize in dealing with foreign direct investors and investments. The results identified four key factors to attract foreign investors. From the research it was made very clear that tourism marketers should use the results of the study in their marketing efforts and that any attempts in formulating any policy to attract FDI should be based on the understanding of what motivates investors to make investments in India. The research has significant contribution towards the identification of motives to this field of knowledge where little research has been conducted despite the known fact that FDI plays such an important role in an economy.

Bibliography

- Asiedo, E. (2002), "On the determinants of foreign direct investment to developing countries: is Africa different?", World Development, Vol. 30 No.1, pp.107-19.
- Bandelj, N. (2002), "Embedded economies: social relations as determinants of foreign direct investment in Central and Eastern Europe", Social Forces, Vol. 81 No.2, pp.409-44.
- Biswas, R. (2002), "Determinants of foreign direct investment", Review of Development Economics, Vol. 6 No.3, pp.492-504.
- Cheng, L.K., Kwan, Y.K. (2000), "What are the determinants of the location of foreign direct investment? The Chinese experience", Journal of International Economics, Vol. 51 No.2, pp.379-400.

- De Mello, L.R. Jr (1997), "Foreign direct investment in developing countries and growth: a selective survey", Journal of Development Studies, Vol. 34 No.1, pp.1-34.
- Eicher, T., Kang, J.W. (2005), "Trade, foreign direct investment or acquisition? Optimal entry modes for multinationals", Journal of Development Economics, Vol. 77 No.1, pp.207-28.
- Ellis, S.M., Steyn, H.S. (2003), "Practical significance (effect sizes) versus or in combination with statistical significance (p-values)", Management Dynamics, Vol. 12 No.4, pp.51-3.
- Francis, J.C. (1993), Management of Investment, 3rd ed., McGraw-Hill, New York, NY, .
- Gray, P.H. (1987), International Economic Problems and Policies, St Martin's Press, New York, NY, .
- Husted, S., Melvin, M. (2004), International Economics, 6th ed., Pearson Education, Pearson/Addison-Wesley, Boston, MA, .
- Lucas, R.E. (1993), "On the determinants of foreign direct investment: evidence from East and South-east Asia", World Development, Vol. 21 No.3, pp.391-406.
- Naudé, W.A., Krugell, W.F. (2003), "Human resource development and foreign direct investment in Africa", unpublished paper prepared for the African Perspectives Yearbook 2003, Institute for World Economics and International Management, University of Bremen, Bremen, .
- Naudé, W.A., Krugell, W.F. (2007), "Investigating geography and institutions as determinants of foreign direct investment in Africa using panel date", Applied Economics, June, Vol. 39 No.10, pp.1223-33.
- Petrochilos, G.A. (1989), Foreign Direct Investment and the Development Process, Gower, Brookfield, VT, .
- Resmini, L. (2000), "The determinants of foreign direct investment in the CEECs: new evidence from sectoral patterns", Economics of Transition, Vol. 8 No.3, pp.665-89.
- Schneider, F., Frey, B.S. (1985), "Economic and political determinants of foreign direct investment", World Development, Vol. 13 No.2, pp.161-75.
- United Nations (UN) (1995), "Sectoral flows of foreign direct investment in Asia and the Pacific", ESCAP Studies in Trade and Development, No.5, pp.17-25.

- Urata, S., Kawai, H. (2000), "The determinants of the location of foreign direct investment by Japanese small and medium-sized enterprises", Small Business Economics, Vol. 15 No.2, pp.79-200.
- Vellas, F., Bécherel, L. (1995), International Tourism: An Economic Perspective, Macmillan, Basingstoke, .
- Veugelers, R. (1991), "Locational determinants and the ranking of host countries: an empirical assessment", Kyklos, Vol. 44 No.3, pp.363-82.
- Wang, Z.Q., Swain, N. (1997), "Determinants of inflow of foreign direct investment in Hungary and China: time-series approach", Journal of International Development, Vol. 9 No.5, pp.695-726.
- Yang, J.Y.Y., Groenewold, N., Tcha, M. (2000), "The determinants of foreign direct investment in Australia", The Economic Record, Vol. 76 No.232, pp.45-54.

FDI in Indian Insurance Sectors: Boon or Bane

Gagan Singh Jaggi

Associate Professor,

Govt. Degree College Nagrota Bagwan, Distt. Kangra (H.P.)

Abstract: One of the premium sectors showing industry upward growth is insurance which a 41 billion US dollar industry in India. In 2011, India was ranked 9th in the life insurance and 19th in the general insurance business globally and is growing at 32% to 34% annually. India is attracting global insurance companies due to its market opportunities. This sector has been thrown open for some 14 years. Before this it was a public sector monopoly. While liberalization of insurance sector, many private life insurance companies were entered with the help of foreign equity up to 26 per cent in the life insurance business. FDI becomes a sensitive issue with arguments from strong both side of debate. As per one view, entry of the more other global players will create more jobs and other services. In other views says that they will displace job instead of creating jobs. But fact is that India cannot avoid global opportunities in this scenario. Foreign Direct Investment is important source of funds. Indian insurance services sector contributing 7 per cent in India's GDP. There is a huge potential growth in future. The insurance sector, by virtue of attracting long term funds, is best placed to channelize long term funds toward the productive sectors of the economy. Therefore the growth in their premium collections is expected to translate into higher investment in other key sectors of the economy. This paper is a study of the impact of FDI in Indian insurance sector.

Keywords: FDI Foreign Direct Investment, GDP Gross Domestic Product, IRDA Insurance Regulatory Development Authority

Introduction:

Investment is an important determinant of economic growth. In general, investment may lead to creation of physical capital, financial capital and human capital. Investment consists of foreign investment and domestic investment. Generally, there are two types of foreign investments involved i.e. Foreign Direct Investment (FDI) and Foreign Portfolio Investment (FPI). Foreign Direct Investment involves the ownership and control of a foreign company in a foreign country. In exchange for the ownership, the investing country usually transfers some of its financial, technical, managerial trademark and other resources to the recipient country. Foreign capital and technology have been playing a vital role in India's industrial development. At the time of Independence, India inherited an industrial structure restricted to a few industries like textiles and sugar. India's exports were stagnant for the first 15 years after independence due to neglect of trade policy by the Indian Government of that period. Since liberalization, the value of India's international trade has increased sharply with the contribution of total trade in goods and services. India accounts for 1.44% of exports and 2.12% of imports for merchandise trade and 3.34% of exports and 3.31% of imports for commercial services trade worldwide India's major trading partners are the European Union, China, the United States of America, and the United Arab Emirates. Today, the industrial structure has been widely diversified covering broadly the entire range of consumer, intermediate and capital goods. In most of the manufactured products, the country has achieved self-sufficiency with foreign collaboration. In 2006-07, major exports commodities included engineering goods, petroleum products, chemical and pharmaceuticals, gems and jewelry, textiles and garments, agriculture products, iron ore and other minerals. Major import commodities included crude oil and related products, machinery, electronic goods, gold and silver. India is founding member of GATT since 1947 and its successor, the WTO. India has been voicing the concerns of the developing world. For instance, India has continued its opposition to the inclusion of such matter as labour and environment issues and other non-tariff barriers ti trade into the World Trade Organization. The main objective of the study is

1. To overview the FDI scenario in India
2. To study the FDI inflow from different countries.
3. To study and analyze the sector wise FDI inflow in India in specific insurance sector.

To achieve the above objective, secondary data is collected and analyzed from various published reports of government of India, UNCTAD reports and DIPP World Investment Report.

Foreign Investment Flows:

Foreign capital and technology have been playing a vital role in India's industrial development. The economic health of the transition countries in Eastern Europe, Russia and Central Asia is well off due to these inputs. Even the communist countries like China have welcomed the foreign investment to make their economies better. Most of the advanced countries of today developed due to the foreign investment. FDI has an important impact on country's trade balance, increasing skill and labour standards, transfer of technology and innovative ideas, skills and the general business climate. FDI also provides opportunity for transfer and, upgrade technology, improves efficiency and quality of services and goods, optimal utilization of human capabilities and natural resources and helps to provide additional jobs

Table -1

Foreign Direct Investment Inflows in India (US $ Million)

Year	Foreign Direct Investment	Foreign Portfolio Investment	Total
1990-91	97	6	103
1991-92	129	4	133
1992-93	315	244	559
1993-94	586	3,567	4153
1994-95	1314	3824	5138
1995-96	2144	2748	4892
1996-97	2821	3312	6133
1997-98	3557	1828	5385
1998-99	2462	-61	2401
1999-00	2155	3026	5181
2000-01	4029	2760	6789
2001-02	6130	2021	8151
2002-03	5035	979	6014
2003-04	4322	11377	15699
2004-05	6051	8315	15366
2005-06	8961	12492	21453
2006-07	22826	7003	29829
2007-08	34362	27271	61633
2008-09	37838	-13855	23,983
2009-10	37763	32376	70139
2010-11	27024	31471	58495

Source: RBI Bulletin, May 2011

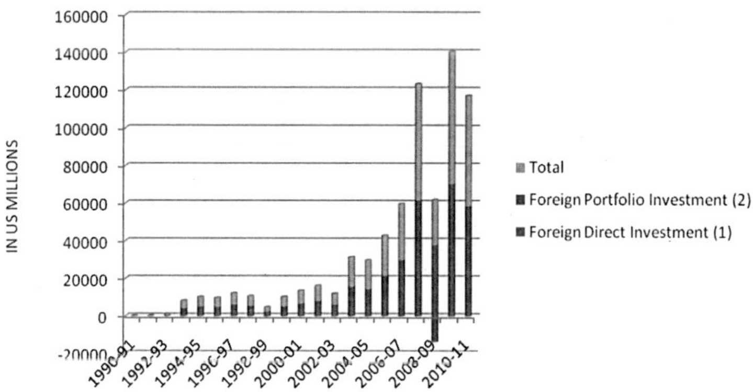

The percentage share of direct foreign investments inflow is found to be more than 27 percent of total foreign investment throughout the study period, except the years 1994 and 1995. The total foreign direct investment of US $415 million in 1992 to inflow of US $27024 million in 2011 is a long journey of 18 years representing a whopping increase of 272.62 times. In 1997 inflow of FDI increased by 21 times touching the figure of US $2821 million, just within its existence of six years, representing 46 percent of total foreign investment of this year. In the year 2000 FDI inflow declined to US $2155 millions due to slow FDI inflow in India. Within a period of next six years its FDI reached the figure of US $5035 million in the year 2003 which was nearly seven times increase. After this, inflow of FDI increased year after year except the year 2004, touching the figure of US $22826 million in the year 2007 representing 76.52 percent of its total

Foreign direct investment (FDI) and foreign portfolio investment (FPI) is considered the form of foreign investment. FDI helps to increase the productive capacity of the economy, while foreign portfolio investment is of a more speculative nature. Table no 1 reveals that during the period 1990-91 to 1994-95, the percentage share of FDI is 24.2 percent of total foreign investment and that of FPI was 75.8 per cent. In other words, only a quarter was very volatile. For the next five years period (1995-96 to 1999-

00), the proportion of FDI in total investment improved to 54.8 per cent. However, year wise data disclosed that fluctuations in foreign portfolio investment were much sharper than those in foreign direct investment (FDI. During the period 1995-96 to 1998-99, FPI has go down from $3,824 million in 1994-95 to a negative level of $61 million in 1998-99, However, it reconverted a level of $3,026 million in 1999-00, this indicates its extreme volatility and revival. Thereafter, again FPI continued to decline and reached a low level of $979 million in 2002-03 the share of FPI which touched a low level of 16,3 per cent in total foreign investment in 2002-03 rose sharply to about 71 per cent in 2003-04. In 2008-09 are find a net outflow if FPI, mainly due to global recession. Obviously, FPI is very undependable. Compared with this situation, the data about FDI shows a gradual upward growth from $129 million in 1991-92 to S1314 million in 1994-95, to further rise to $3,557 million in 1997-98. Subsequently we find increase in FDI in leaps and bounds to $37763 million$ by 2009-10. During 2010-11 there was a decline in FDI in flow to $27024 million. It implies that as a matter of policy, the host country can depend on a regular inflow of FDI if it creates a conductive climate for the purpose.

Country Wise FDI Inflow in India

India lacked a policy of its own on foreign capital pre-independence because it derived its faith in total laissez faire from the British government. Consequently, foreign enterprises found it convenient to export products to India and were justified by local circumstances to setup branches or wholly owned subsidiaries

Table- 2

Country Wise FDI Inflows Top Ten Countries in Recent Years (Rs Crore)

S. No	Countries	2008-09	2009-10	2010-11
1	Mauritius	50794 (41.28)	49633 (40.2)	31855 (35.99)

S. No	Countries	2008-09	2009-10	2010-11
2	Singapore	15727 (12.78)	11295 (9.15)	7730 (8.73)
3	USA	8002 (6.50)	9230 (7.48)	5353 (6.04)
4	UK	3840 (3.12)	3094 (2.51)	3434 (3.88)
5	Netherland	3922 (3.19)	4283 (3.47)	5501 (6.21)
6	Japan	1889 (1.53)	5670 (4.60)	7063 (7.98)
7	Cyprus	5983 (4.86)	7728 (6.26)	4171 (4.71)
8	Germany	2750 (2.24)	2980 (2.41)	908 (1.02)
9	France	2098 (1.70)	1437 (1.16)	3349 (3.78)
10	UAE	1133 (0.92)	3017 (2.45)	1569 (1.77)
	Total FDI	123025	123378	88520

Source-DIPP Ministry of Commerce FDI statistics 2008-11

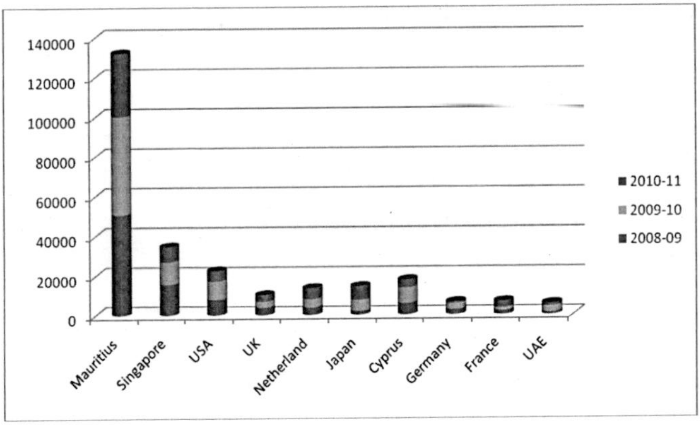

The analysis of country wise inflows of FDI in India from different countries during 2008-09 to 2010-11 adds to a total amount of Rs 334923 crores received from the countries. From the above table and diagram, we observed that Mauritius has been the largest direct investor in India, which stand first with a total inflow of Rs 50794 crores in the year 2008-09. Although this amount was considerably decreased to Rs 31855 crore in 2010-11 but still Mauritius is on the top among foreign investors in India. The Singapore is the second largest investor in India. The total capital flows from USA was around 7730 crore, which accounted for 8.73 percent of the FDI inflows. United State America and United Kingdom are India's third and fourth largest FDI inflows. On the other hand Mauritius was recorded with highest inflow of 41.28 % in the year 2008-09 which showed declining trend till 2010-11 but remained on first position. Same trend is observed in case of other countries over the period analyzed.

Sectoral Analysis of FDI in India:

It is observed from the table that services sector has attracted largest amount of foreign direct investment during the recent period of 2000-2010. This sector has attracted the foreign direct investment of 100692 crores that equals 19.42 percent of the total foreign direct investment flows. It is followed by computer software and hardware sector whose share has been increased during the same period. This sector has attracted 11.12 percent of the total foreign direct investment flows. The telecommunication sector has received foreign direct investment of 42620 crore which is the 7.40 percent of the total flows of foreign direct investment. The foreign direct investment of Petroleum and natural gas, and chemical and Fertilizers are 12026 crores and 11390 crores respectively.

Table-3

Analysis of Top Ten Sectors in India in Recent Years (Rs Crore)

Sector	2008-09	2009-10	2010-11	Cumulative Inflows (2000-2010)
Service	28411	20958	15539	106992
Computer Software	7329	4350	3571	44611
Telecommunication	11327	12338	7546	42620
Housing and Real Estate	12621	13586	5149	37615
Construction	8792	13544	5077	36066
Power	4382	6908	6088	21466
Automobile	5212	5609	5709	20864
Metallurgical	4157	1935	5055	13845
Petroleum and natural gas	1931	1328	2621	12026
Chemical & fertilizers	3427	1707	1810	11390

Source:-Department of Industrial Policy and Promotion (DIPP)

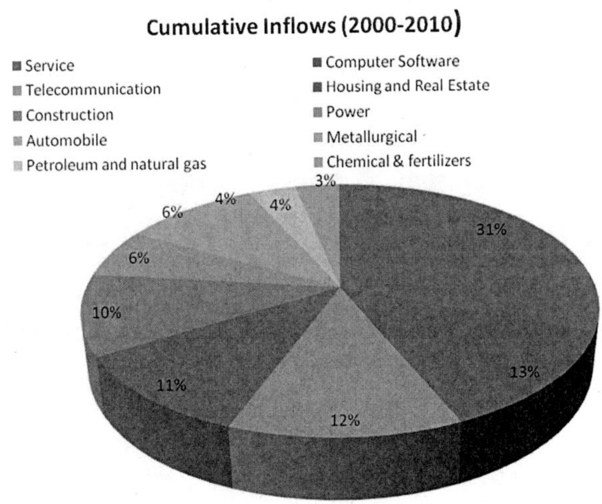

Table-4

Ranking of Sector Wise FDI Inflows in India Since April 2000- Dec 2010

Sector	Rank
Service Sector	1
Computer Hardware and Software	2
Telecommunication	3
Housing and Real Estate	4
Construction Activities	5
Power	6
Automobile Industry	7
Metallurgical Industry	8
Petroleum and Natural Gas	9
Chemicals	10

Source: Department of Industrial Policies and Promotions.

The Sector wise Analysis of FDI Inflow in India reveals that maximum FDI has taken place in the service sector including the telecommunication, information technology, travel and many others. The service sector is followed by the computer hardware and software in terms of FDI. High volumes of FDI take place in telecommunication, real estate, construction, power, automobiles, etc. The rapid development of the telecommunication sector was due to the FDI inflows in form of international players entering the market and transfer of advanced technologies. The telecom industry is one of the fastest growing industries in India. With a growth rate of 45%, Indian telecom industry has the highest growth rate in the world. FDI inflows to real estate sector in India have developed the sector. The increased flow of foreign direct investment in the real estate sector in India has helped in the growth, development, and expansion of the sector. India has become one of the most prime destinations in terms of construction activities as well as real estate investment. The FDI in the automobile sector in India ranks third in manufacturing three wheelers and second in manufacturing of two wheelers. Opportunities of FDI in the Automobile Sector in India exist in establishing Engineering Centres, Two Wheeler Segment, Exports, Establishing Research and Development Centres, Heavy truck Segment, Passenger Car Segment. The increased FDI Inflows to Metallurgical Industries in India has helped to bring in the latest technology to the industries. Further the increased FDI Inflows to Metallurgical Industries in India has led to the development, expansion, and growth of the industries. All this has helped in improving the quality of the products of the metallurgical industries in India. The increased flow of foreign direct investment in the chemicals industry in India has helped in the development, expansion, and growth of the industry. It is observed from the above table that top ten sectors attract almost 70 % of FDI inflows. Thus the sector wise inflows of FDI in India shows a varying trend but acts as a catalyst for growth, quality maintenance and development of Indian Industries to a greater and larger extend. The technology transfer is also seen as one of the major change apart from increase in operational efficiency, managerial efficiency, employment opportunities and infrastructure development

FDI and Insurance Sector In India – An Overview:

Indian insurance sector got liberalized in 2001. Since then the sector has grown at 20% annually and have seen entry of 41 private insurance companies (Life: 23, General: 18) with many of them choosing to enter with a foreign joint venture partner. Investment through the FDI can be a maximum of 26%. In 2011, India was ranked 9th in life insurance business and 19th in general insurance business globally. The insurance density stood at USD 64.4 (USD 9.9 in 2001) and insurance penetration was 5.2% (2.3% in 2001).India has 49 life and general insurance companies with total investment of USD 6 Bn. as of March 2011..9With the deregulation of insurance industry in India since 1999, private players have got an opportunity to enter in an insurance markets. Prior to its deregulation, the life insurance business was dominated by the public sector company is life insurance Corporation of India. While liberalization of insurance sector, as many as twelve new private life insurance companies were entered with the help of foreign equity up to 26 per cent in the life insurance business apart from the HDFC standard life, which has stand foreign equity only 18.6% in the beginning of insurance business, The importance of FDI in the development of a capital deficient country such as India cannot be undermined. This is where the high-growth sectors of an economy play an important role by attracting substantial foreign investments. Currently, the total FDI in the insurance sector, which was Rs. 50.3 billion at the end of financial year 2009, is estimated to increase to approximately Rs. 61 billion in financial year 2012. The insurance sector, by virtue of attracting long-term funds, is best placed to channelize long-term funds toward the productive sectors of the economy. Therefore, the growth in their premium collections is expected to translate into higher investments in other key sectors of the economy. Therefore, the liberalization of FDI norms for insurance would not only benefit the sector, but several other critical sectors of the economy.

Life Insurance Industry Overview:

The Life insurance companies are the most trusted financial service providers. Life insurance is an emotional and a highly serious business which is mainly attributed to achieve a social cause.It is the opportune time to the insurance companies after liberalization to play an appreciable role in doing insurance business and making the task of insuring people more efficient and customer-friendly. Indian life insurance industry is a dynamic industry wherein different functions, structures and inter-relationships are to be taken care of. Life insurance sector plays an important role in providing risk cover, investment and tax planning for individuals. The life insurance sector grew at an impressive CAGR of 25.8% between financial year 2003 and financial year 2009 and the number of policies issued increased at a CAGR of 12.3% during the same period. As of August 2010, there were 23 players in the sector (1 public and 22 private). The Life Insurance Corporation of India (LIC) is the only public sector player, and held almost 65% of the market share in financial year (based on first-year premiums). To address the need for highly customized products and ensure prompt service, a large number of private sector players have entered the market. MetLife, ICICI Prudential Life Insurance, Bajaj Allianz Life, Max Life Insurance, Sahara Life Insurance, Tata AIG Life, HDFC Standard Life, Birla Sun life, Kotak Life Insurance, Aviva Life Insurance, Reliance Life Insurance Company Limited, LIC ING Vysya Life Insurance, Shriram Life Insurance, Bharti AXA Life Insurance Co Ltd, Future General Life Insurance Co Ltd, IDBI Federal Life Insurance, AEGON Religare Life Insurance, DLF Pramerica Life Insurance, CANARA HSBC Oriental Bank Of Commerce Life Insurance, India First Generali Life Insurance Company, and Star Union Life Insurance Co. Ltd, Star Union Dia-ichi Life Insurance Co. Ltd. Innovative products, aggressive marketing and effective distribution have enabled fledgling private insurance companies to sign up Indian customers more rapidly than expected. Private sector players are expected to play an increasingly important role in the growth of the insurance sector in the near future. The existing smaller players have aggressive plans for network expansion as their foreign partners are keen to capitalize on the enormous potential that is latent in the Indian life insurance market. ICICI Prudential, Bajaj Allianz and SBI Life collectively account for approximately 50% of the market share in the private life insurance segment. To tap this opportunity, banks have also started entering alliances with insurance companies to develop/underwrite insurance products rather than merely distribute them. HDFC standard Life Insurance Company Limited was the first private insurer registered with the IRDA and India First Life Insurance Company Limited was the last private insurer registered with the Regulator.

Table: 5
Market Share Amongst Private Players – Financial Year 2010

S. No.	Private Players	Market Share (in %)
1	Bajaj Allianz	11.6
2	Met Life	2.8
3	SBI Life	18.3
4	ICICI Prudential	16.5
5	Tata AIG	3.4
6	Kotak Mohindra	3.5
7	MNYL	4.8
8	HDFC Standard	8.6
9	Birla Sunlife	7.7
10	Reliance	10.2
11	Others	8.6
12	New entrants	4.0
	Total	100.00

Source: IRDA Annual Report 2009-10

Non-Life Insurance Industry Overview:

The non-life insurance industry provides a risk cover for assets. Health insurance and pension systems are fundamental to protecting individuals against the hazards of life, and India, as the second-most populous nation in the world, offers significant potential for that type of cover. Furthermore, fire and liability insurance are essential for corporations to safeguard infrastructure projects and investment risks. Between financial year 2003 and financial year 2010, the non-life insurance sector grew at a CAGR of 17.05%. Intense competition that followed the de-tariffication and pricing deregulation (which was started during financial year 2007) decelerated the growth momentum. As of August 2010, the sector had a total of 24 players (6 public insurers, 17 private insurers and 1 re-insurer). The non-life insurance sector offers products such as auto insurance, health insurance, fire insurance and marine insurance, aviation insurance, engineering, personal accidents, liability etc. Private sector players have now pivoted their focus on auto and health sector. Out of the total non-life insurance premiums during financial year 2010, auto insurance accounted for 43.5% of the market share. The health insurance segment has posted the highest growth, with its share in the total non-life insurance portfolio increasing from 12.8% in FY07 to 20.8% in FY10.

Table: 6

Market Share Amongst Private Players – Financial Year 2010

S. No.	Private Players	Market Share (in %)
1	Royal Sundram	2.4
2	HDFC ERGO General	2.4
3	Star Health and Allied Insurance	2.6
4	AIC	4.0
5	IFFCO-Tokyo	4.3
6	ICICI-Lombard	8.6
7	National	12.1
8	Oriental	12.4
9	New India	15.7
10	Bajaj Allianz	6.6
11	United India	13.6
12	Reliance General	5.2
13	Tata-AIG	2.4
14	Others	7.9
	Total	100.0

Source: IRDA Annual Report 2009-10

Contribution of Insurance Sector to Employment:

Insurance has had a very positive impact on India's economic development. The sector is gradually increasing its contribution to the country's GDP. In addition, insurance is driving the infrastructure sector by increasing investments each year. Further, insurance has boosted the employment scenario in India by providing direct as well as indirect employment opportunities.

Table-7

Growing Employment in The Life Insurance Industry

Parameter	2006	2007	2008	2009
Direct Employees	1,52,449	1,87,403	2,54,332	2,85,244
Individual Agents	14,22,609	19,85,457	24,98,513	29,06,281
Total	1575058	2172860	2752845	3191525

Source: Life Insurance Council of India

Insurance helps create both direct and indirect employment in the economy. Alongside regular jobs in insurance, there is always demand for a range of associated professionals such as brokers, insurance advisors, agents, underwriters, claims managers and actuaries. The increasing insurance business has increased the demand for highly skilled professionals as well as semiskilled and unskilled people. This table depicts that the life insurance provided direct employment to an additional set of 30,912 people during financial year 2009, besides adding more than 407,768 individual agents during financial year 2009. IRDA has mandated the appointment of actuaries in all insurance companies, ensuring the certification of all products before launch. The insurance regulator has also made it mandatory for appointed actuaries to attend all board meetings to help the insurer ensure solvency at all points in time. To ensure continued growth, the need of the hour is trained manpower with specialized knowledge about this industry. Insurances companies need to invest in the professional training of their employees, especially for subjects such as underwriting, claims and risk management.

Opportunities of Allowing Foreign Direct Investment in Insurance Sector:

- Opening up of insurance sector for FDI also has some positive impact on the economy. The insurance sector is best placed to channelize long-term funds toward the productive sectors of the economy. Therefore, the growth in their premium collections is expected to translate into higher investments in other key sectors of the economy. Therefore, the liberalization of FDI norms for insurance would not only benefit the sector, but several other critical sectors of the economy.
- The total revenues from the Indian off shore insurance business process outsourcing services has also increased from year to year (US$ 367 million in financial 2003 to US$ 790 million in financial year 2007) and are expected to reach US$2 billion by financial year 2010. This increased business will also result in increased employment opportunities in the insurance off shoring business.
- Technology of foreign players will be brought in country through FDI. This will help to provide better service, delivery also reduce costs. Institutions can also strengthen their ties with customers and differentiate themselves from competition. In addition, there is significant potential in the micro-insurance segment with the majority of the Indian population residing in rural areas.
- Through FDI, The distribution networks have reached an unprecedented scale from mobile phone companies to micro finance institutions to supermarket chains and churches. Customers, in vast numbers, who were previously off the grid, are now within reach.
- Global insurer will bring best management practices in Indian insurance sector. The expansion into new markets

is expected to help drive profits, as developed economies witness slower growth in the demand for insurance

Advantages of Allowing FDI In Insurance Sector

- At present, there are 23 life insurance companies operating in the country. Competition among the insurance players provides the impetus for rapid growth. The insurance sector is a big one and is growing at a rapid pace ranging between 15 to 20 per cent. Along with banking services, insurance services add about 7 per cent to the country's GDP. The private players have been trying to reach out to rural masses by a paradigm shift in the focus of insurance from class insurance to mass insurance. Regional Rural Banks and Co-operative Banks assist the insurance players to have a rural touch, local feel and a familiarity with rural economy. In totality, the operation of private insurers in India has benefited our insurance system by enhancing competition and efficiency. A well-conceived and developed insurance sector is a gift to any country for its economic development since it provides long-term funds for infrastructure development and strengthening the risk-taking ability of the country. Opening up of Indian insurance sector for FDI will also have some positive impact on the economy. But government has to be very careful about it.
- One of the advantages of foreign direct investment is that it helps in the economic development of the particular country where the investment is being made.
- Foreign direct investment helps in the creation of new jobs in a particular country.
- It becomes easier for the business entities to borrow finance at lesser rates of interest. The biggest beneficiaries of these facilities are the small and medium-sized business enterprises.
- The growth of FDI in India boosted the economic growth of the country. Major advantages of FDI in India have been in terms of -

- Increased capital flow.
- Improved technology.
- Management expertise.
- Access to international markets.
- Contribution to export growth

Disadvantages of Allowing FDI in Insurance Sector:

- A higher foreign direct investment (FDI) will unshackle the insurance industry and drive growth and long-term development, enrich the business by bringing world-class business practices and processes, expand distribution capabilities and deepen market penetration.
- Over Rs 10,000 crore of foreign capital could flow into the country if the Government were to pass the Insurance Amendment Bill that raises the FDI limit. More players in the market would increase the flow of more money in the market which would have impact on the economic drivers of the country.
- Inflation rates would have an impact due to the heavy load of money in the country. Government has to take measures to control it.
- Creation of monopoly is biggest threat posed by private players.

Recommendations for the Industry and Government

- FDI in India is important source of fund. It cannot be avoided for long hence indian government must make adequate FDI policies in advance about insurance sector.
- Government intervention whenever is necessary.
- Government must make insurance policies for global insurance companies regarding employment of locals, infrastructure policies and other fields, so that economic development cannot be hamper.

- Indian multinationals must be encouraged to enter insurance sectors so that global players have stiff competitions to face and monopoly cannot be created in Indian market.

Conclusion

Governments of the superior countries like the U.S. continue to apply stress on developing countries to open up their insurance sectors. China, for instance was pressurized to open up its insurance sector, in return of its entry into the WTO. However the strong countries dictate the terms to the developing countries and FDI would help in countries to grow and know the potential of the country and find out a target market for the product or service been offered. The more stake of FDI in the country would have a very great impact on the economic conditions of the country. The outlook for the general insurance industry in India is stable based on steady fundamental credit conditions in the sector over the next 12-18 months. With the Indian economy forecast to grow at 9% in 2010 and given rising income levels and higher risk awareness among insured, the country's insurers are optimistic about demand for their products. However, intense competition from new entrants, deregulation and a moderation in returns from the equities market will pressure pricing and ultimately short-term profitability. At the same time, despite rising inflation and a severe correction in the stock market, the prevailing view in Asia is that while China and India are not insulated from the credit crisis afflicting the US and EU, domestic demand is strong enough to support GDP growth. But until the existing insurance players show substantial benefits or it addresses the issues at hand, there would not be much of value addition to the country.

References:

1) Hema Gupta, Sudhi Gupta and Naresh Aggarwal, "Growth of Life Insurance Sector" Insurance Chronicle, The ICFAI University Press, May 2004, pp 25-29

2) Russell, I. Parera, "Privatisation of Insurance – Challenges and Opportunities" The Chartered Accontant, Jan 2001, p 24.

3) World Investment Report UNCTAD , 2011

4) DIPP Report on FDI ministry of commerce Govt. of India

5) Vepa Kamasam and Padmavathi, "Challenging Task- CSR For Insurance Sector"IRDA Journal, Jan., 2011, p 33.

6) Annual Report of LIC.Indian Economy 2011, S Chand company, New DelhiIndia 2012 Programmes and policies Nov 2011 chronicle

7) Business Economics Globe India UK Nov 2011The Indian economy unique publishers New DelhiReforms 2020 The Financial Express Nov 2011

RBI handbook of statistics on Indian economy2009-10

http//www.igovernment.in/site/FDI-in-India-insurance-sector-to-be-raised-to-49

http;//www.banknetindia.com/banking/80928.htm

http;//www.irdaindia.org

www.sodhgangainflibnet, org.